Ryan Sport Trainer

by

Dorr B. Carpenter

Ryan Sport Trainer

by

Dorr B. Carpenter

Published as part of the
"Aviation Heritage Library Series"

by
SunShine House, Inc.
P.O. Box 2065
Terre Haute, IN 47802
(812) 232-3076

Ryan Sport Trainer

by

Dorr B. Carpenter

Published as part of the
"Aviation Heritage Library Series"
by

SunShine House
P.O. Box 2065
Terre Haute, IN 47802

First Edition, First Printing
Printed in the United States of America

Library of Congress
Catalog Card Number 90-70983

ISBN 0-943691-03-6

The book is the fifth in The Aviation Heritage Library Series published by SunShine House, Inc.
Drina Welch Abel
Alan Abel

The Aviation Heritage Library Series is published to preserve, for future generations, the history of the men and women, and of their airplanes, during the era of the Golden Years of Aviation.

The Aviation Heritage Library Series:
First book: ***The Welch Airplane Story*** by Drina Welch Abel
Second book: ***It's a Funk!*** by G. Dale Beach
Third book: ***The Luscombe Story*** by John C. Swick
Fourth book: ***The Earhart Disappearance - The British Connection*** by James A. Donahue
Fifth book: ***Ryan Sport Trainer*** by Dorr B. Carpenter

Front and back photo credit: Chris Woods

Contents

About the Author
Dorr B. Carpenter

This is Dorr Carpenter's third Ryan book. This book fills the gap of the Ryan ST in photographs and information between his other two books, *On Wings of Cloth* and *Ryan Guidebook.*

Dorr has over 950 hours in Ryan airplanes and those he has owned include one PT-22 and ST series airplanes c/n 355, 104, 198, 476, 456, and 177. This airplane (c/n 177) is on display at the San Diego Aerospace Museum.

Dorr's licenses include Commercial Pilot with Instrument Rating; a DC-3 Type Rating; and an A & P. He is an FAA and IA Inspector.

In addition to his three Ryan books, he also has authored more than 35 aviation magazine articles and is the author of another book, *Submarines of Japan's Imperial Navy, 1904-1945.*

The author is married and father of three children. He graduated in 1951 from St. Lawrence University (Canton, N.Y.) and served in the military in Korea with the rank of infantry lieutenant.

Dorr and his wife, Elizabeth, reside in Virginia.

AVIATION HERITAGE RESEARCH CENTER

T. Claude Ryan

January 3, 1898 - September 11, 1982

Foreword

by William Wagner
Vice President
Ryan Aeronautical Company

Aviation has taken some mighty strides in the last 65 years, few more lengthy than those of the concerns founded by T. Claude Ryan, who began in 1922 with a discarded Army Jenny, a cracker-box office, and an "airport" distinguished by a runway of dubious utility.

From this modest start has grown an organization of international prestige, Teledyne Ryan Aeronautical. In its formative years, the company built military planes and parts, and its affiliate, the Ryan School of Aeronautics, trained hundreds of army pilots for World War II at San Diego and Hemet, California, and Tucson, Arizona.

Ryan, who in 1982 celebrated the 60th anniversary of his obscure entrance into commercial aviation, was one of that early, carefree group of pilots who learned to fly by the seat of their pants. His boyhood days at Parsons, Kansas, where he was born January 3, 1898, were spent mooning at fanciful stories and articles about flying, though he actually did not see a plane until the fall of 1911, when Cal P. Rodgers flew over the Kansas hamlet in his Wright Model B biplane while making the first transcontinental plane flight.

The Armistice of 1918 snagged Ryan's ambition to fly for Uncle Sam in the war zone, but he had in the meanwhile obtained some idea of how to operate a plane at a flight school in Venice, California, after his folks moved to southern California. The school, like many of its kind in those years when aviation was more swashbuckling romance than business, had wobbly financing and wobblier equipment, and although Claude had deposited $500.00 for 400 minutes—yes, minutes—of instruction, his training in solo flying consisted of a hop 30 feet into the air, and a somewhat abrupt landing that resulted in a broken propeller. The cost of fixing the prop, $75.00, was beyond the school's financial capacity, and it simply sagged out of existence.

Ryan eventually was successful in enrolling for training as an army cadet at March Field, California, in the fall of 1919, when Brig. Gen. Barton K. Yount, later head of the Air Force Flying Command, was in charge of that air station. Among Claude's cadet classmates were men later to win fame in pioneering airlines, such as "Jimmie" James and Fred Kelly of Western Air Express as well as many like Major Lowell Smith who made reputations as officers in the Army Air Corps.

Completing a tour of active service as a flying officer in January 1922, after duty that included patrolling the forest fire area of northern California and Oregon, Ryan tried his hand at various activities, only to find that his heart was still in aviation. He came to Rockwell Field, "cradle" of army aviation in San Diego, to fly on his Reserve commission, when the "break" occurred that unalterably swerved him into a career of teaching flying, operating airline schedules and manufacturing planes.

He learned that a pilot flying passengers from a runway at the foot of San Diego's Broadway, near the waterfront, had involuntarily abandoned the enterprise. It appeared that the law had overtaken him in the act of smuggling Chinese across the border, had convicted him, and had sent him away for quite a while to think it over.

It didn't take Claude Ryan long to clinch a deal with the Harbor Department of the City of San Diego for use of that field; a little longer to bargain with the Army at Rockwell Field for a Jenny which it was about to get rid of, anyway. He now waited for business, and it was slow in arriving. For six months, he took off and landed with a relative handful of passengers, maneuvering under high-tension electric wires, between poles at the end of his runway and near a mast on a dredge in the bay nearby.

It was far from an ideal situation, so Claude moved farther up the harbor to the salt flats, later known as Ryan Airport, where the "Spirit of St. Louis" took off on its maiden test flight in 1927 after its manufacture by the Ryan organization, and where other notable events in Ryan's history took place. Another Jenny was acquired, and Ryan now was able to refer to his activity as the Ryan Flying Company since the organization had by then grown to a size worthy of such a title.

When the government in 1923 offered for sale its wartime flying equipment at bargain rates, Ryan bid a few hundred dollars on six Standard biplanes and spare parts to be shipped from Texas. It was the step that, unknowingly at the time, was to turn Ryan toward manufacturing. For when the planes arrived, they were in such dreadful condition that Claude and his mechanics began a major redesigning and rebuilding job. Working with Ryan on this first "production" task were Hawley Bowlus, later one of the nation's leading sailplane experts, John Van Der Linde and Dan Burnett, important production executives of the Ryan Aeronautical Company, and Martin Jensen, famed for an early flight to Hawaii.

The two-place open cockpit planes emerged as five seater Ryan-Standard cabin ships, equipped with 150 hp Hispano-Suiza engines. With these planes, Ryan built a well-paying sightseeing business. From this to expanding his flight instruction work was a natural step.

One of Ryan's early students was B. F. Mahoney, a well-to-do sportsman pilot who proposed an association with Claude in a passenger-carrying venture between San Diego and Los Angeles. Fees of $29.50 for the round trip journey and $17.50 for a one-way flight were set, and on March 1, 1925, Ryan Airlines, Inc., first year-around passenger airline in the United States, began shuttling between two major cities of southern California.

Seeking a plane for the "Los Angeles-San Diego Line" with larger passenger capacity than those on hand, Ryan came across one of Donald Douglas' first experiments in the aircraft field, the famed Cloudster. The continually redesigning Ryan converted the craft from one to three open cockpits to a cabin ship capable of carrying 10 passengers, in addition to the pilot and mechanic or co-pilot. Forerunner of the modern airlines, the new Cloudster had passenger accommodations almost equal to the much later Boeing 247.

By the time the Cloudster was rebuilt, the Ryan shops had taken on virtual factory status, and Ryan sought to launch a design conceived and built in his own organization. The result was the M-1, a high-wing monoplane able to carry an 800 pound load and cruise at 115 miles per hour. The de Havilland planes, then in use, carried the mail for the U.S. Postal Service and held less than half that load. Vern C. Gorst, who was later awarded the first air-mail contract on the Pacific Coast, a night scheduled run between Los Angeles and Seattle, depended from the inception of his rather ambitious plan on Claude Ryan for technical advice and the operational setup of the airline. Result of this collaboration was Pacific Air Transport, which was later to became the Pacific Division of United Air Lines.

Gorst contracted with Ryan for a fleet of Ryan M-1 mail planes equipped with Wright J-4 Whirlwind engines. Preceding the sale of the first planes to Pacific Air Transport, Claude Ryan personally piloted the first Ryan M-1 mail plane with Vern Gorst as passenger on an aerial survey of the Los Angeles-Seattle route. With a full cargo and flying most of the way at 10,000 feet, Ryan shattered inter-city records en-route in a phenomenal performance.

At Vancouver, Washington, a special D-H, flown by U.S. Army ace Lt. Oakley Kelly, first to fly across the nation non-stop, was pitted against Ryan's M-1 in a challenge race that attracted widespread attention. The M-1's neat triumph proved the turning point in the career of Claude Ryan as a manufacturer. It gave him the orders for planes from contract air mail lines—Pacific Air Transport, Colorado Airways and Clifford Ball Airlines—and the zest for production that never left him.

The M-1 was improved into a later version, the M-2, and Ryan then reached another milestone in his upward climb, the design and production of the "Bluebird", his first cabin monoplane. He demonstrated he was only at the start of his unceasing efforts to better his product, and later revisions resulted in an advanced type cabin ship known as the B-1.

The first Ryan B-1 Brougham, built in 1926, was sold to the late Frank Hawks, speed burner of his day. The M-1 and the "Bluebird" had made national reputations virtually overnight and late in 1926, after Claude had sold his interest in the original manufacturing company to his partner but consented to remain four months as manager, a fateful telegram arrived from the Robertson Aircraft Corp. of St. Louis, which asked in effect:

"Can you build a plane with a Wright Whirlwind J-5 engine, capable of flying nonstop New York to Paris?"

Shortly after Ryan's affirmative reply, a lanky ex-airmail pilot named Charles Lindbergh put in an appearance at the Ryan airport. He was the pilot Robertson had in mind for this hazardous venture. In 60 days, the "Spirit of St. Louis" was completed, and Lindbergh left San Diego on the first leg of the flight that proved the adrenaline shot aviation had needed.

Ryan went to Europe in 1928 on a combination honeymoon and business trip, as U. S. sales and manufacturing representative of the Siemens-Halske radial air-cooled engines, but he later disposed of his agency and returned to San Diego, ready to resume the uphill climb to leadership in the industry.

The Ryan Aeronautical Company, keystone of the Ryan group, was incorporated in 1931, when the depression was making itself bitterly felt. But serenely confident of the future of aviation, Ryan built administration and school buildings and hangars, and then undertook development of the world-renowned ST low-wing metal-fuselaged sport trainer.

For the Army Air Corps during World War II, Ryan trained 14,000 pilots most of whom received their primary instruction in ST-type Ryan PT-22 military trainers.

Also, during WWII, the company designed and built Navy jet-plus-propeller Ryan FR-1 Fireball carrier-based fighters. In later years Ryan developed a variety of vertical takeoff and landing (VTOL) research aircraft.

And, for the past 40 years, Ryan has been the premier builder of remotely-piloted target drone and reconnaissance jet aircraft (RPVs) including 'spy planes' used in the Southeast Asia in the late 1960s.

First flight of the Sport Trainer, June 8, 1934, Model ST-1, c/n 101, NX14223. RYAN

T. Claude Ryan and Bill "Doc" Sloan with an STA in 1938. RYAN

Introduction

by William "Doc" Sloan
San Diego, California

One of the far-visioned aviation pioneers and the man most responsible for the first really successful low-wing sport aircraft was T. Claude Ryan. As president of the Ryan Aeronautical Company, located at San Diego, California, he was not a dreamer. He was one of those magnificent men who was not only a pilot's pilot, but a solid businessman, a designer without benefit of formal education, and a man with a keen insight to create aircraft one jump ahead of the state-of-the-art.

Converting surplus WW I trainers into passenger-carrying aircraft was his first step. In 1927, with Charlie Lindbergh at the controls of a Ryan built monoplane flying the Atlantic solo, aviation grew from the heroic dare-devil status to the greatest method of transportation the world has ever experienced.

In the late thirties, there weren't many fixed base operators making a reliable living. Charter trips provided some income, but flight instruction was the bread-and-butter item that kept them going. The old Wacos, the Travel Airs, Aeroncas, Taylorcrafts, Cubs and the Great Lakes were the prevalent trainers. More than fifty years ago, in 1932, Claude, with his uncanny ability to look ahead, employed Millard Boyd, a young engineer, to refine his concept of a design for a low-wing, streamlined trainer that would be safe, reliable, and capable of meeting the training requirements for pilots entering the age of aircraft which flew more than two hundred miles an hour. As a hangover from the barnstorming days, it was called "sport," and with an eye to the future, he labeled it "trainer." Thus, the "ST" was christened to become the Ryan Sport Trainer.

The market for such an aircraft was limited. Most fixed base operators weren't renown for a financial status that would allow purchasing up-to-date trainers. The U. S. government was then buying antique Consolidated PT-1s and a few Stearman

(Left to right) Harry Cameron, Capt. Malcolm Stewart and Bill Sloan prior to delivery of three Ryan STM aircraft to Honduras. RYAN

PT-13 biplanes, but it was some of the trouble-shrouded smaller countries that kept the ST in production. The Chinese Air Force, under attack from the Japanese; Java, under the threat of being overrun, Mexico, Guatemala, and Honduras in Central America—these were the aviation-conscious, air-minded countries that sent in orders for limited quantities of potential fighter-trainers that kept the production line going.

Another boost for the development of the airplane was the "sportsman-pilot." As an accredited flight school in San Diego where the weather permitted year round training and an escape from the frozen north, many of the wealthy kids from the east sought flying instruction which included training in the most up-to-date trainer in the country. The climate, the professionalism of the Ryan instructors, and the excitement of a modern airplane added to the financial backing that kept the production line going.

I soloed at Ryan in the Great Lakes biplane. Possibly it was the best of the old two-wing trainers. Forgiving, soft to land and no unexpected ground-looping tendencies, she was more than passable in aerobatics. The inverted 90 hp Cirrus engine was known to shed exhaust stacks occasionally, but if treated with due respect and an understanding of her occasional unreliability, she was a pleasure to fly.

It was shortly after earning my private license that I was allowed to fly my first ST, NC 17353. The transition from an antiquated biplane to a low-winged modern airplane was like jumping from antiquity into a new world. After five hours of careful supervision, Verne Murdock and Paul Wilcox turned me loose to solo the ST. The training in that sleek, fast aircraft stayed with me for the next thirty years.

It had taken nearly four years of design, redesign, engine changes and a lot of guts to give birth to the ST in which I soloed. Johnny Fornasero did all of the initial testing on the unproved airframe. The original configuration was too blunt and boxy to satisfy Claude. Millard Boyd finally redesigned the cowl to cover the streamlined engine, adding a longer, more graceful wing which gave the bird the sum total of beauty-of-line and perfection of detail which Claude demanded. After several short flights which showed less than promising results, a new prop was installed on the 95 hp Menasco, and the ST was born. Approved Type Certificate #541 was issued and the ST was on its way to becoming the most popular sport trainer of the decade.

After over 50 years, the Ryan Sport Trainer is still a classic. Webster defines a classic as being "of recognized value; serving a standard of excellence; traditional and enduring; characterized by simple tailored lines in fashion year after year." The ST meets all of these criteria.

Yet, why can this still-young slip of a girl excite the imagination of any pilot who has ever flown her? First, it wasn't just simply herding a mass of aluminum through the sky. It was an experience of one-ness with the freedom from the earth and a truly responsive machine that responded affectionately to every touch of the controls. Admittedly, the cockpit was crowded after donning flight suits, cushions or chutes and boots, but the feeling persisted that you didn't fly the airplane—you wore it.

Putting in honest hours and gaining experience is the first step to becoming a qualified pilot. Once I had received my transport ticket I was partially on the way, but lack of experience, money and offers from airlines for a young aspirant led me to accept (expenses only) the pleasant chore of flying check-pilot on advanced school cross-country flights for yet-to-be qualified students.

We flew STs from San Diego to San Francisco, Las Vegas, Tucson, Monterey and Los Angeles in those by-gone days when there was no radar, air traffic controllers or enforced regulations prohibiting freedom of exhilarating flight. As an "experienced" pilot, it was a joy to ride the front cockpit, get safely from point A to B, and encourage the fledgling in the back seat to become proficient. The real euphoria, however, was flying the ST.

In 1938 the Honduran government purchased three STMs to augment their growing air force. Malcolm Stewart, an old guy of thirty-some years and a Randolph/Kelly graduate, soldier of fortune and ex-Captain in the U. S. Air Corps, was Chief of the Honduran Air Force. His newest assignment was to deliver three STMs to Honduras. He hired Rod Cameron—ex-barnstormer and savvy pilot from Los Angeles and Doc Sloan, a young kid with 200 hours under his belt, to join him in ferrying the new ships to Honduras.

It took two weeks to make the flight from San Diego to Tegucigalpa, Honduras, and that kid matured considerably during that period. We flew through unbelievably bad weather, crossed jungles marked "unexplored" on our primitive charts, and slow rolled down the main drag of the capital to increase the Honduran Air Force by ten percent.

The STMs were equipped with the Menasco C4S 150 hp supercharged engine which gave us an honest 130 mph cruise. With the front cockpit cowled in to hold another 30 gallon gas tank, we had nearly a 600 mile range. Slightly touchy on takeoff because of the torque generated by the additional horsepower, the STM was a symphony of grace, maneuverability and unrestricted joy.

Several noted authors and aviation buffs have

written books describing the Ryan history. Bill Wagner's *Ryan, the Aviator* and his *Lightning Bugs* are outstanding examples. The Carpenter/Mayborn *Ryan Guidebook* is a fine addition to those publications. Dorr Carpenter's *The Ryan Sport Trainer* will become an interesting historical document about one of the finest aircraft ever built.

Fortunately, I had the opportunity to know Claude Ryan for over forty years. Never satisfied with the newest design, he continually reached out for the next step in promoting his love of aviation. He went quietly in 1982 at the age of 84. Sitting in his study, working over the design for private aircraft yet to come, he went West after a lifelong contribution to the promotion of aviation.

There was much more to his life than the production of the Sport Trainer, but it was one of his happiest and most gratifying flying machines. He was able to fly the STM as a kid of 74, and the fortunate few who own them today will still experience the joy of being sky-borne in a beautiful airplane.

Individuals who helped make this book possible:

Bill Allen
D. J. Armand
Glen Buffington
Gerard Casino
Bill Dodd
Ernest Gann
Bill Hodges
Burton Kemp
Leo Kohn
Ted Koston
Paul Matt
Mitch Mayborn
William Richards
William "Doc" Sloan
William Wagner
James Young

RYAN

The Sport Trainer team. From left to right, Johnny Fornasero, T. Claude Ryan, Millard Boyd and Will Vandermeer.

Chapter One

The shop crew and the prototype Sport Trainer, c/n 101, that they built. Standing on the right are Hawley Bowlus, airframe foreman, and James Fornasero, engine foreman, with Johnny Fornasero in the cockpit. RYAN

The Sport Trainer Model-1 (ST-1)

The first Sport Trainer completed carried construction number (c/n) 101 and cost $1,000 to engineer. The entire project was accomplished—including design, drawing, building, test flying and certification—in nine months. This figure is derived by examination of the original factory blueprints; the earliest date that was found was September 12, 1933, and the first test flight was the following June.

Chief pilot John B. Fornasero flew the sleek prototype X14223 for the first time on June 8, 1934. A very long and laborious takeoff was required and after a few test turns, Fornasero was back on the ground within ten minutes.

The problem seemed to be the propeller, which was a Story ground adjustable aluminum blade model. It was replaced with a wooden one and the problem was solved. It was not realized until some time later that the 95 hp Menasco B4 engine was insufficient. Only five of the B4 powered models were built: c/ns 101, 102, 104, 117, and 155 between 1934 and 1937.

After just two weeks of testing at Mines Field in Los Angeles, the ST was granted ATC 541 on June 21, 1934. The "New Ryan" was used for flight instruction and promotional purposes, while the second and third airplanes were under construction. A student, Sanford Baldwin, was flying NC14223 on December 19, 1934, when it crashed, killing the pilot. The accident was witnessed by U. S. Navy Captain John Tower, who reported that the continuing aerobatics were so low the pilot simply was unable to complete the maneuver. This was the first fatal accident in twelve years of Ryan School operations.

To continue operations, Claude Ryan needed additional financing and it was obtained from a stock sale to the father of Ryan student Johnny Funk, in 1935. In the meantime, the second ST, c/n 102, NC14909, was delivered personally by T. Claude Ryan to Leonard R. Peterson in Seattle, Washington. Unfortunately, it crashed at Pesco, Washington, sometime later after being sold to E. Weller.

The price for the Sport Trainer was quite reasonable. The 95 hp model sold at first for only $3,985, or, taken as a package deal with training for an Airline Transport license, for $4,642. By 1937, the ST was up to $4,185—without any kind of pilot training.

The first STA, NC14910, carried c/n 103 and was completed on April 21, 1935. The difference was basically in the engine, which had more power and provided a great improvement over the underpowered ST. The original engine used was the Menasco C4 of 125 hp, but the ATC also allowed the installation of the Menasco D4 of equal horsepower. This model carried ATC 571, granted May 23, 1935. A total of 71 aircraft were built from 1935-1940. In 1935, 26 were sold at $4,685 each, and in 1936, 34 at $4,585.

Peter Dana bought the first STA with a package deal, including flying lessons. After learning to fly, he set a number of inter-city speed records. He flew from San Diego to New York in 25 hours, 40 minutes and then did it again in 22 hours, 6 minutes, beating his own record. He also established a "Tri-Flag" record from Vancouver, B. C., to Tijuana, Mexico, in 11 hours and 6 minutes.

NC14910 and NC14911 were used at Palwaukee, Illinois, by Tufts Edgcombe in a 1942 Naval officers flight program. Three such classes were held, and when the course ended, NC14910 was sold. Her sister ship, however, had a very bad reputation as being temperamental and squirrelly and a very difficult ship to sell.

Dan Cardinal, an instructor at the time, tells of NC14911's last flight. "She was rented to a student who made a very low approach to land and almost hit a hangar. At the last moment he pulled up but stalled fifty feet up and crashed in a large cloud of dust. This solved the problem of what to do with that cranky

Ed Goetz, Les Comce, Bud Wilner, Dick Nelson, and Jim Brough with NC14910 at Palwaukee, Illinois. DAN CARDINAL

Ryan STB, only one was built without front seat and with a long range fuel tank. Note: experimental wing root fairing and cowl louvers. This was a special order for sportsman Cliff Durant.

RYAN

Ryan." The pilot was unhurt.

The Ryan Sport Trainer attracted a great deal of attention, particularly when John "Tex" Rankin was at the controls. He flew a stock STA, c/n 107, NC14914, owned by the Ryan Aeronautical Company, and became a Ryan salesman. Unfortunately, he did not stop flying long enough during a typical barnstorming tour.

"Tex" phoned Ryan one Sunday morning. "Claude, you'll never believe what happened to me," he blurted. "I was taking off to demonstrate the airplane at Detroit and, believe this or not, the rudder fell off! Now don't get excited, the airplane's okay. I didn't crack up. But you know something? That airplane you fellows designed is so stable and so controllable I didn't need a rudder. I flew it with the ailerons and elevator and made a perfect landing with no trouble at all."

STA, c/n 108, NC14952, was the first to be crated and shipped out of the country. It went to Honolulu, Hawaii, July 39, 1935, but was wrecked shortly thereafter.

One Ryan STB, c/n 109, NC14953, was built. It was a special order for sportsman Cliff Durant and

Tex Rankin and Ryan NC16039.

WAGNER

featured a long range fuel tank in place of the front seat. Powered by a Menasco C4, 125 hp and delivered November 6, 1935, it was later converted to a standard two seater STA January 27, 1938. It was destroyed in an accident at Sacramento, California, in 1939.

Rankin flew his own STA, NC16039, equipped with a stock C4 engine in the International Aerobatic Competition at St. Louis on Memorial Day 1937. He placed first, ahead of the biplanes that had ruled the competition ever since they were instigated. Tex did modify the propeller and as a result got much higher rpm's from the engine.

Gladys O'Donnell used Rankin's Ryan in the Amelia Earhart Trophy Races of 1936 and 1937. They were handicap events, the latter one being a Memorial race, since Amelia Earhart had disappeared in July of that year. The race in 1936 was a 40-mile event flown at Los Angeles where O'Donnell placed second in NC16039 and Genevieve Savage was third in another unidentified Ryan/Menasco aircraft. The 1937 event was flown at the Cleveland National Air Races and was a 25-mile, five lap event. Gladys O'Donnell won in 11:34 minutes with a speed of 120.653 mph. (NC16039 was still flying in California as late as 1976). O'Donnell was again involved with Ryans at the Primary Air Corps Training Detachment at Visalia-Dinuba Field during WW II.

Rankin and "Put" Humphreys flew for Bob Wilson's "Hollywood Air Aces" in the mid-1930s. (Humphreys used the Ryan, while Rankin used a Great Lakes during their exhibition.) The Ryan's advanced design was a crowd pleaser.

By January 1936, most STs sold were purchased individually. However, W. H. Irwin of Atlanta, Georgia, wanted to set up a distributorship and talked in terms of fifteen aircraft, but sales records show only eight were ultimately sold through him. His offer included negotiable bonds to finance increased production and, at one point, actually made a threat with a six-gun to ensure completion of the deal! Years later, Claude Ryan said of the incident, "I never did get myself involved with those bonds where I couldn't produce them, because I remember that six-shooter."

The first STA-Spl was c/n 121 and was completed April 30, 1936, NC16031. Approximately 34 were built, and again, they were basically the same airframe but equipped with the 150 hp Menasco C4S supercharged engine. They carried ATC 681 and all the civilian models were manufactured between 1936 and 1939. It is particularly important to note the number produced, because in 1976 more STA-Spls were flying in America than were originally built!

All the military STM aircraft returned to this country fall under this old ATC. Only two of the original civilian STA-Spls remain—c/n 188, NC18904, and c/n 339, NC18921. The 1936 price was $5,185. This may seem low, but they really were not. In the mid-thirties a new "De Luxe" Ford automobile could be bought for $850. When this is projected and compared to a new Ford of today, the price of the Ryan STA-Spl would have to have been $51,850.

Ryan STA-Spl, c/n 141, was originally sold through dealer Ted Brown, and registered in the U. S. as NC17307. It was known to have been damaged severely on September 1, 1939, and then removed from the civil register.

While in Nicaragua in 1955, the author saw what is believed to be this old Ryan still in use by the National Guard officers for training and sport. Capt. Juergen Sengelman, N.A.F.R., the officer who befriended me in Nicaragua earlier, responding to my 1970 inquiry about the plane wrote, "The Nicaraguan Air Force does not have the Ryan aircraft mentioned. This particular plane made a forced landing in the lake (Menagua) several years back and it was never recuperated." Recently a question has been raised as to what plane this really was. The other possibility is that it is c/n 181, NC18903, which had its registration cancelled and was shipped out of the U. S. in April 1940.

NC17345 landing at the Chicago Amphitheater for the International Air Show, 1938. ART SHELTER

My Personal Interest with the ST

The International Air Show held at the Chicago Amphitheater in January 1938 is an unforgettable event for me. My father took me, as a boy of nine, to see all the airplanes, but I could only see one. It was hanging from the ceiling as if flying in a gentle dive. The most gorgeous, shining, beautiful thing I had ever seen—a Ryan STA. There was a second Ryan on the floor, but I hardly noticed it. One of the airplanes was c/n 148, NC17345, owned by Art Shelter who operated the old Sky Harbor Airport north of Chicago. Even more remarkable was the news that the planes had been flown in and landed on the parking lot!

In 1967, after a fine restoration, this same Ryan was flown around the east coast area and then in Florida where it was sold twice in a very short period of time. The new owner, in his sixties and only recently recovered from a heart attack, started the ferry flight from Florida to his home in Ohio. He never made it and died at the controls over Georgia. The old Ryan flew itself for a time and landed in the tree tops, only falling to the ground after forward motion had stopped. The wreck was sold to John Gokchoff in California who is very well known for his modified Ryans. He partially restored the aircraft and then sold it to John Crouse of Virginia. (Flying in 1986).

Bill Joy was a Ryan distributor in Detroit and in 1937, he sent his son, Tom, to learn flying at the Ryan School. Tom bought the package deal—Transport Pilots Course and aircraft.

In 1976, William Wagner said, "Anyway, after completing his course, Tom and a friend flew to Santa Monica one day. Though he had no instrument training, Tom took off in a heavy cloud-fog cover and spun in. Of course, he'd been taught not to take on instrument weather without instrument training." He was not flying his own aircraft at the time; the plane was c/n 163, NC17358.

A story about c/n 164, originally a Ryan School aircraft, is quoted from a letter by Mitch Mayborn. "Ryan STA Special, c/n 164, NC17359, has been a puzzle to those of us who have followed the histories of the various STA airplanes. For one thing, it was carried on the FAA license rolls up until the mid-1970s. Rumor has it that the plane was stolen from the owner, A. R. Cuellars of San Diego, Texas, and he left it registered in case it turned up. While the exact events are unknown, the true story can now be told.

"It seems about 1955 (plus or minus a year or so), the airplane was either loaned or rented to a local pilot at Alice, Texas, who either had an engine failure or misjudged a buzz job and crashed at George West. The damaged plane was returned to Alice. George Smith, an old time aviator and FBO at Alice, was the gentleman to whom I talked and who gave me this information. He was also the man who asked to rebuild the airplane. At the time he said it would cost more than it was worth and so the airplane was dragged out to the junk heap and left. The engine was removed and sold. During the mid-1960s, the local junk dealer picked up the fuselage and it is now a pot or pan! Sad story about the end of a fine airplane."

Harry Marshall, an advanced student at the Ryan School in 1938, was severely injured in his STA, c/n 178, NC16037. His Ryan had been modified with an inverted fuel system and smoke to make trails while doing aerobatics. The short exhaust stacks on the Menasco cannot be adapted to smoke without an extensive collector and a long exhaust pipe. The back pressure will otherwise stop the engine, as it did on NC16037 while it was on its back at 100 feet over the desert practice area known as Camp Kerney. The ship stalled when rolling over and crashed. Marshall died about six months later after only a partial recovery.

Open sport planes, particularly the ST Ryans, are conducive to questionable behavior. Pilots who otherwise fly in a very sedate manner will strap on a Ryan and act like a big kid. There are almost no exceptions to this. This is the only airplane I have ever flown that will forgive you for nearly any foolishness, given reasonable altitude. None have ever come apart in the air, and they are universally liked by all pilots except those who had to fly one in the winter.

There is no question that this is an emotional airplane; even sitting on the ground it is a symbol of speed, grace and beauty. Granted, I am not impartial as I have had the feeling of being sorry for other pilots, while preparing my Ryan STA for a flight, because most of them just don't know what it is to fly a really good sport airplane.

Hollywood did not miss the opportunity to feature the Ryan in a number of now classic movies. The STA was a "British fighter" in the film *Dive Bomber* starring Fred MacMurray and Errol Flynn. Walter Pidgeon and Clark Gable made a 1938 film with Myrna Loy called *Too Hot To Handle* with an STA used as a news-camera plane. Another was *Test Pilot,* with Myrna Loy, Clark Gable and Spencer Tracy. *Fighter Squadron* depicted two Ryans camouflaged to resemble retractable gear fighters. Those of us who were kids in the thirties thrilled to the adventures of Howie Wing with his STA, NC17300, a Saturday afternoon radio special.

Edward Bowman has owned NC17353 for many years. He and the Ryan had a small incident in 1965 involving the metal tip of a propeller blade. The tip flew off and Ed thought he had the emergency landing under control. He shut down the engine because of the high vibrations, but he came up short of the field and the Ryan was damaged. It was subsequently stored.

Another Ryan STA was found in the base-

Ryan School aircraft NC17359, c/n 164, with red tail and stripe. Most of the school's aircraft had a different colored tail and stripe. Note the school insignia on the fuselage. JAMES YOUNG

ment of a Chicago apartment house in 1965. It had been stored after having been flown over 3200 hours. Used in many training programs; some pages of the log book showed month after month with five and six hours a day in the air. The really surprising aspect is that in all this time there was not even a broken propeller. The first 3150 hours were flown with the original engine. Eight log books and three major overhauls later, this same Menasco D4 was acquired with the aircraft, crated in good condition by another party. This fine old ship needed only paint and cover to put it back in the air.

Dario Toffenetti bought it and flew it from 1967-1975. A number of mishaps occurred over the years, but nothing serious. Toffenetti and his Ryan won several awards, including the T. Claude Ryan trophy for the "Most Original Ryan ST" at Ottumwa, Iowa, in 1975. I bought it in November '75 with a broken prop and a bent rudder when it went on its back for the first time.

NC17364, c/n 177, is the highest time Ryan known, with 3350 hours in the air. The logs which go back to 1943 show three hard ground loops and three times on its back.

Russell Brown from Kansas bought it in almost derelict condition and spent

(Left) Clark Gable and Myrna Loy with an STA on the set for Too Hot To Handle, *1938.*

CARPENTER

E. E. Hilbert, pilot and D. Toffentti, co-pilot in Ryan STA, c/n 164, NC17361, with Norman Denis in PT-21, N52456, in the foreground. Photo taken in September, 1967.

STA-Spl c/n 180 built for the National Advisory Committee for Aeronautics. RYAN

ten years putting it back in first class shape. His work forced him to relocate from Kansas to Ohio with the plane finished, except for painting. The ferry flight was never completed. The propeller bolts failed and Russ made a dead stick landing into a "clear" field. The unseen fence literally tore the Ryan to pieces. The pilot was not hurt. The second restoration took nine months and was completed in June, 1974. It now flies in Illinois and is the fastest STA I have ever known.

Laura Ingalls purchased c/n 179, NC18901, in June, 1938. The plane was equipped at the factory with an inverted fuel system for aerobatics. It is unfortunate that this well known aviatrix did not use this STA to set any of her many aviation records. The last owner was the Troy Flying Service, Troy, New York. The plane crashed in 1944, killing both student and instructor.

The National Advisory Committee for Aeronautics, Langley Field, purchased STA-Spl, c/n 180, for research purposes. Licensed NACA-96, it was flown east from the factory in September, 1938. Little is known of how it was used, but an indication could be derived from a photo caption in Aviation magazine in 1939, showing a wing fitted with flaps that are similar to Fowler flaps on modern jet aircraft. The caption read, "Split, extendable flap resembling a Zap flap was tested by NACA on research program on increased lift."

A Ryan advertisement of the period had this to say: "This type of plane was apparently chosen by NACA because it is the only plane of its size which has

Ryan STA c/n 177, NC17364, in 1974. CARPENTER

NC9 as a CAA pilot check plane at St. Louis. Note the old Mahoney Aircraft Corp. building in the background. The year was 1940. BURTON KEMP

transport plane operation characteristics." This aircraft was sold by the government testing agency and re-registered as N180Y, but has not been licensed for years.

Demorr Aviation of New York purchased c/n 198, NC18902, in September, 1938. As is usually the case, it had a number of owners and was used as a trainer during the war, this time by the Navy Indoctrination Program at the University of Georgia. It and a sister Ryan were flipped on their backs at the Athens Airport in June, 1943, by a tornado.

A CAA supervisor, Charles J. Adalf, bought c/n 198 and operated it along with several other Ryans over a number of years. In 1946 a Connecticut boy obtained it and planned to see the country from the Ryan's open cockpit. He got as far as Panama City, Florida, when the Menasco quit on takeoff over the ocean. He crash landed in shallow water with little damage and no injuries to himself.

Walter Shebee, a Rhode Island aircraft dealer, purchased the remains and stored the fuselage in his barn and the wings and tail in the chicken coop. Years passed and when space was needed, the fuselage spent the next 17 years "out back in the woods." Bullet holes, ground squirrels, and rust made short work of the aluminum and steel parts. In the meantime, the coop's roof fell on the wings.

Little was left but some good ailerons, flaps, and bulkheads of the original aircraft when I purchased the unidentified parts in 1966. After careful cleaning, the number 198 was found on #2 bulkhead and number 179 on the left wing. With extreme good fortune, the original papers and logs were obtained from the boy, now Lt. Col. Arthur McEwen, U.S.A.F.

Parts from a number of other Ryans were used to rebuild this STA. The tail came from c/n 104, an engine from Canada, and the gas tank from an unknown Ryan in Connecticut. Six months later on June 10, 1967, it flew again with her original registration NC18902.

The fame of this fine aircraft had spread over most of the world by the 1940s and Ryan STs were in use in such countries as South Africa, Venezuela, Brazil, Bolivia, Ecuador, Mexico, Honduras, Guatemala, Nicaragua, Australia, Java, Chile and Argentina.

The 201-299 range of construction numbers was not used for ST aircraft, but was reserved for the SC—Sport Cabin planes. This is sometimes confusing and unexpected because there was an STA-Spl, c/n 200, NC18906.

A very important factor concerning the availability of Menasco engines today resulted from the decision by the Royal Canadian Air Force to buy 200 of them in 1941. They were originally procured, but rarely used, for Tiger Moth aircraft as a replacement for the D. H. Gipsy 145 hp engine used in the Moth. Most were D4-87, although some were D4s.

They were stored throughout the war and then sold surplus in 1946. This resulted in numerous inexpensive engines and has kept the price down until recently. In poor condition, they now sell for $2,000-5,000 and in new shape with logs and crated, for about $8,000.

This is not the case for C4S engines for which there is no supply. These engines in poor condition go for around $3,000. Good or overhauled ones sell for $9,000 and up. Even the old C4 is now worth something because a few parts are interchangeable with the C4S.

Leonard Povey, while working for the CAA, took delivery of N9, c/n 355, at the factory and flew it to St. Louis in March, 1940. It was the last civilian STA built and, although many Model-2 STs were built before, it was a Model-1. This was also the case for c/n 312 which, along with 355, were the only Model-1 aircraft in the civilian group that were manufactured with enlarged cockpit openings.

Number 355's registration number was changed to NC9E when the government sold it. This was a very well known STA, as it was registered almost every year from 1940-1967. The logs show trips to Canada, Mexico, and the Bahama Islands with up to 200 mile trips over water. In April 1965 it hit a bird which split the propeller. It landed safely, only to have a tornado collapse a hangar on top of it that same day. After repairs, NC9E flew east to storage in Virginia.

An experimental STK, c/n 406, NX18924, was used by the factory to test the air cooled radial Kinner B5 engine for possible use on military trainers. The experimental license on file with the CAA states the purpose was to "determine engine suitability." When the tests were completed and the Kinner engine accepted for use on PT-16A and 20A aircraft conversions, the airplane disappeared. There is no record of its having been sold, wrecked or scrapped.

There are only two reasonable assumptions to the mystery. It either went to China, because serial numbers on both sides of it were assigned to China contracts, or it became a PT-20. This latter theory is based on the fact that PT-20 stenciling is visible on the fuselage and "V" strut in a photograph.

The late forties saw the price of a good flying ST drop to a low of $900. This was the period when flight schools were using relatively newer surplus aircraft and the latest production cabin planes. As the demand and interest dropped so did the quality of maintenance, and many STs just sat tied down outside to deteriorate until they were scrapped.

It was not until the late 1950s and early 1960s that the price started to go up. In 1964 I paid $4,200 for NC9E in poor, but flying, condition. The early 1970s saw the figure up to about $10,000 with prices of the supercharged ST-1 model slightly higher. For a reason that is not fully understood, the military model-2 aircraft from Australia do not demand the same high interest and price that the Guatemalan STM Ryan, or the civilian planes do. In general, the Aussi Ryans are lower time aircraft and much more convenient to handle with their toe brakes.

The Ryan STA was originally certified for only the C4 and D4 engines. More recently, because of the availability of the D4-87 engine, they were unofficially accepted for installation on these aircraft, when in fact, they were nine hp more powerful. There is no reason why they should not be acceptable, as both D4 and D4-87 engines are totally interchangeable on the Ryan aircraft and both engines are certified ATC 67.

No Ryan ST series aircraft have type certificates allowing installation of either floats or skis. Whether or not this was an oversight by the factory is not known. The facts are that 48 STM-S2 (STA-Spl-2) were equipped with floats for foreign use and did admirable service with the possible exception of having poor spin characteristics.

One question that has always been asked and cannot be answered, except with opinions and personal preferences is, "Which was best, the Kinner B5 or the Menasco C4 engine?"

The Menascos were replaced by Kinners in the military, and the Army preferred radial engines for training aircraft. Kinners were known to have weak master rods while Menascos had weak valves. Both engines had the same Army recommended overhaul time. Unfortunately, not enough actual samples of individual engines and their service records are available to answer this question, once and for all. The facts at hand indicate the Kinner was a good military engine and a second rate sport plane engine. The Menasco, on the other hand, was a good sport plane engine and a poor military one.

Ryan PT-20, July 3, 1940. U. S. AIR FORCE

XPT-16, formally NC18907, c/n 306. This was the first aircraft ever bought by the U.S. Government from Ryan Aeronautical Company. RYAN

Ryan ST-A shot at Ithaca, New York with early engine cowl louvers. HAROLD ANDREWS

GENERAL SPECIFICATIONS
ST-A, MENASCO C-4, 125 hp ENGINE

WEIGHT EMPTY	1,035 lbs.
USEFUL LOAD	565 lbs.
GROSS WEIGHT (MAX.)	1,600 lbs.
MAXIMUM SPEED AT S.L.	150 mph
CRUISING SPEED AT 2,000 FT.	127 mph
RANGE AT CRUISE	380 miles
CLIMB AT S.L. (MAX. EFFORT)	1,200 ft./min.
SERVICE CEILING	17,500 feet
LANDING SPEED, WITH FLAPS	60 mph
LANDING SPEED, FLAPS UP	70 mph
TAKEOFF RUN, FULL LOAD	175 yards
WING AREA	124 sq. ft.
POWER LOADING	12.8 lbs./hp
WING LOADING	12.9 lbs/sq. ft.

POWER - MENASCO C-4 FOUR CYLINDER INVERTED INLINE AIRCOOLED ENGINE RATED 125 H.P. AT 2,175 RPM

NOTE:
NC14985, c/n 117 WAS BUILT AS A 95 H.P. MENASCO B-4 POWERED ST MODEL ORIGINALLY. IT BECAME AN ST-A LATER WHEN A 125 H.P. MENASCO D-4 ENGINE WAS INSTALLED.

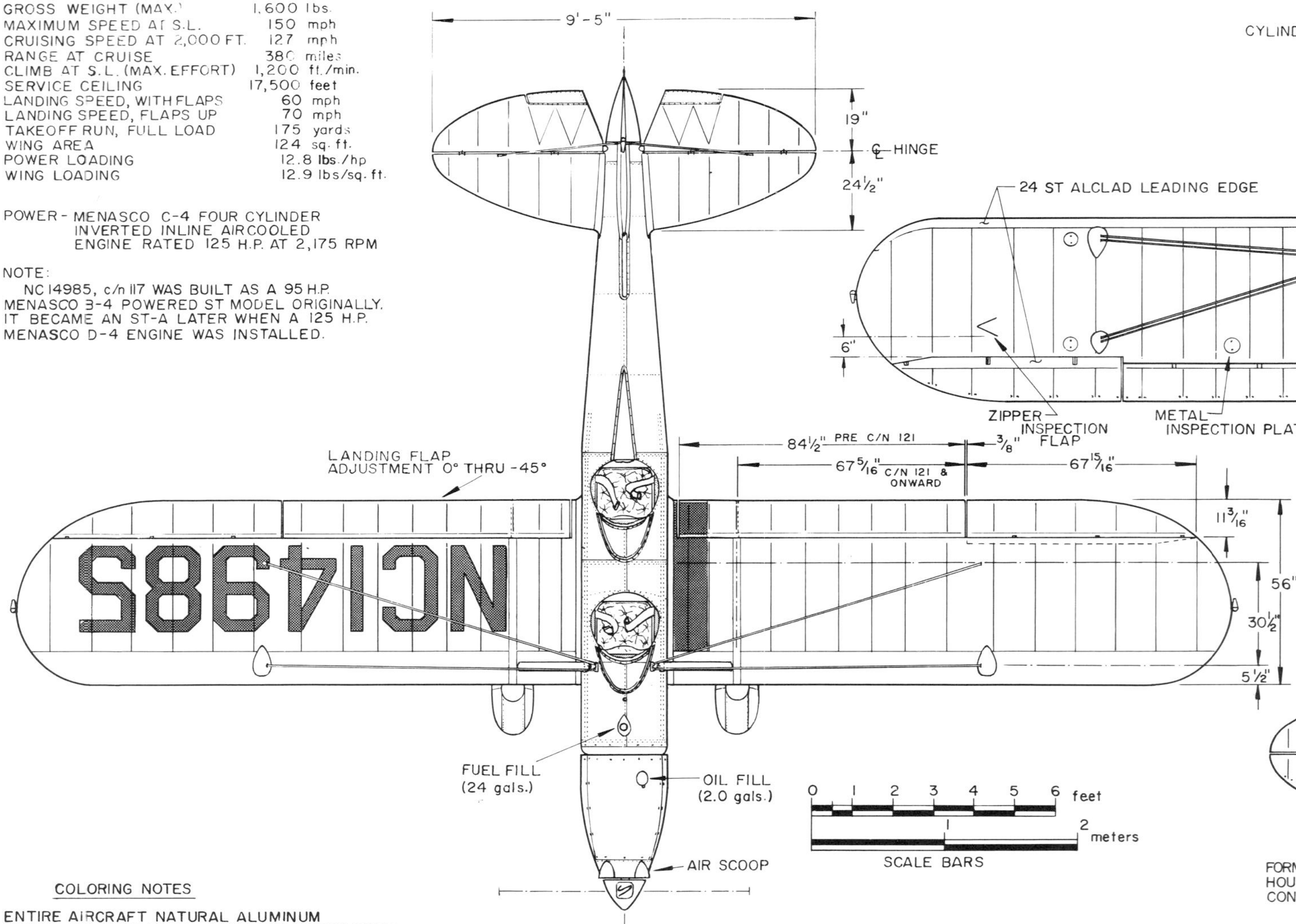

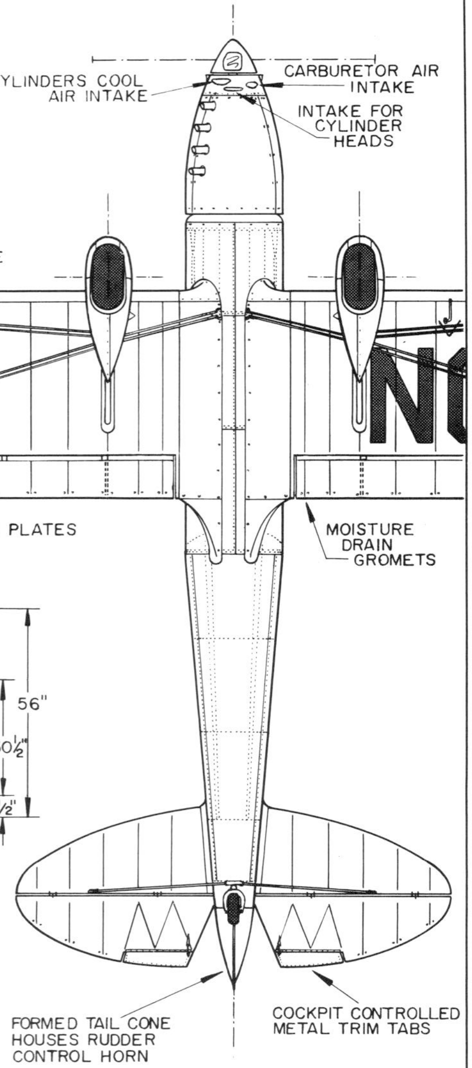

SCALE BARS: 0 1 2 3 4 5 6 feet; 1 2 meters

COLORING NOTES

ENTIRE AIRCRAFT NATURAL ALUMINUM
FABRIC COVERED AREA, MATCHING SILVER DOPE
LICENSE NUMBERS & DETAILS, BLACK
INTERIOR OF COCKPIT AREA UPHOLSTERED IN RED OR BLACK LEATHERETTE, INSTRUMENT PANEL BLACK "CRINKLE" FINISH, CONTROL STICK AND WING FLAP CONTROL LEVER CHROME PLATED.

MY SINCERE APPRECIATION IS EXTENDED TO MESSERS. T. CLAUDE RYAN, WILLIAM WAGNER, AND MAC CATRELL OF THE RYAN AERONAUTICAL CORP., EV. CASSAGNERES AND FLOYD CARTER FOR THEIR VALUABLE AND UNSELFISH HELP IN THE PREPARATION OF THESE DRAWINGS

CONSTRUCTION NOTES

FUSELAGE - ALL METAL, MONOCOQUE, ALCLAD 24 ST SKIN.
WINGS - SPRUCE SPARS, STAMPED ALUMINUM ALLOY RIBS, STEEL TUBE COMPRESSION MEMBERS, STEEL CABLE TIE LINES, FABRIC COVERED.
AILERONS & WING FLAPS - STEEL TUBE SPAR, ALUMINUM ALLOY RIBS, FABRIC COVERED.
TAIL SURFACES - RIVETED 24 ST ALUMINUM TUBING AND ALLOY RIBS, FABRIC COVERED.

DRAWING No. 9-76-A

PLATE 1 of 2

HISTORICAL AVIATION ALBUM

RYAN ST-A
c/n 117 NC14985
1936

SCALE - ORIGINAL 1:24
REPRO. 1:48
DRAWN BY - PAUL R. MATT

SunShine House, Inc. • P.O. Box 2065
Terre Haute, IN 47802

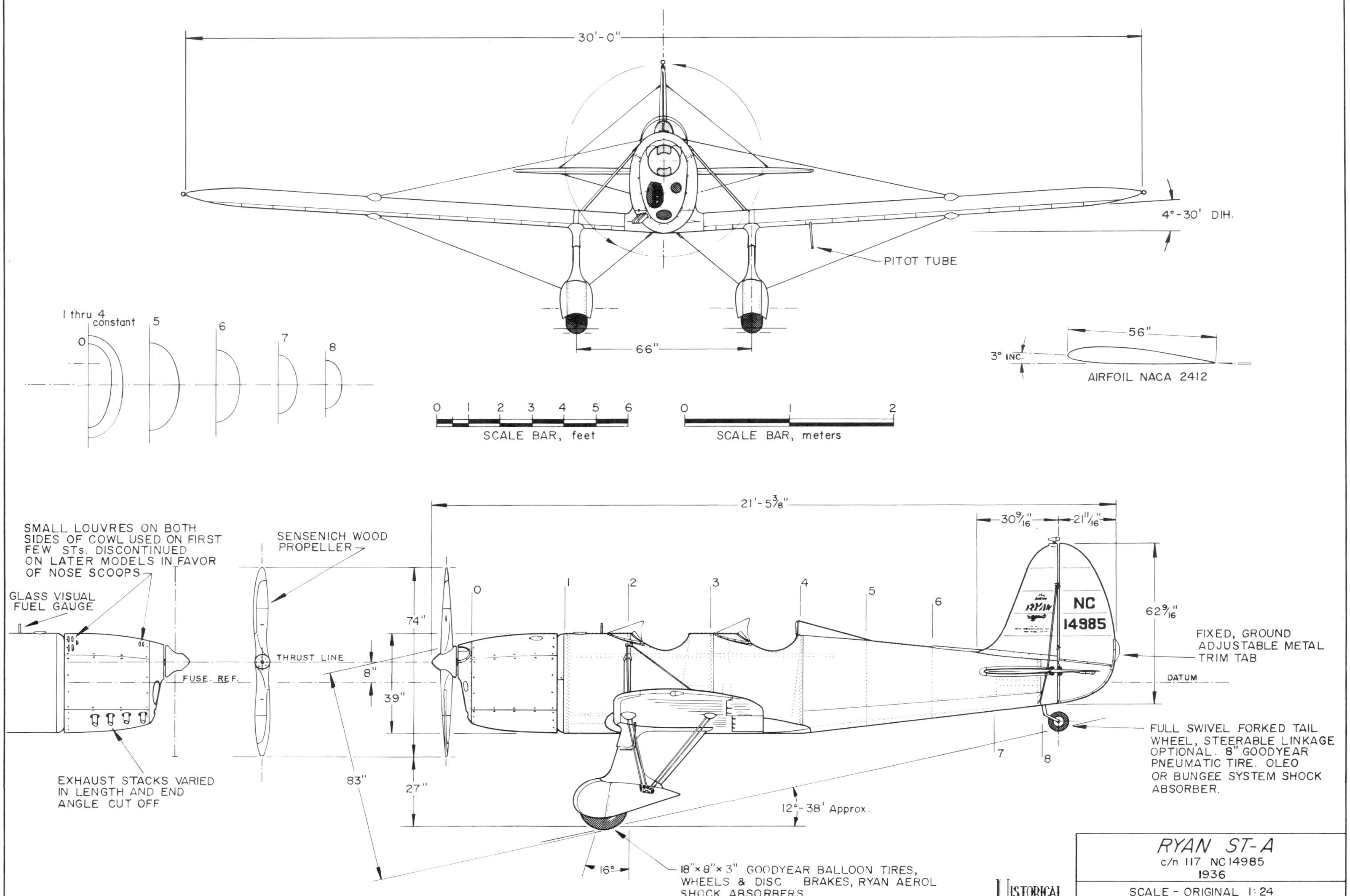

HISTORICAL AVIATION ALBUM

DRAWING No. 9-76-A

PLATE 2 of 2

RYAN ST-A
c/n 117 NC14985
1936

SCALE - ORIGINAL 1:24
REPRO. 1:48

DRAWN BY - PAUL R. MATT

BILL YEAGER

ART SHELTER

(Above) Ryan STA with factory built winter enclosure.

(Left) Art Shelter, Chicago area Ryan dealer (left), and NC17345, c/n 148, at Sky Harbor, Illinois, about 1939.

(Below) STW experimental tests of the Warner engines. Shown is NX18919, c/n 338.

JAMES YOUNG

Chapter Two

STM-S2 in the markings of the Dutch Navy with twin Edo floats. Test aircraft airborn over San Diego. RYAN

STM Aircraft

Advertised as "light fighters" and trainers, the STMs were sold to numerous countries in the late 1930s. The STM-1 (Sport Trainer Military Model One) were all powered by the 150 hp Menasco (C4S) engines and could operate from fields of high elevation because of their superchargers. All were built in accordance to the civilian type certificate for STA-Spl, ATC 681. A small percentage were equipped with machine guns.

No basic difference existed in these early military aircraft from their civilian counterparts. About all that was added were crank starters and the insignia of the country to which it was sold.

Mexico was first to order the STMs on December 9, 1937. They were unarmed with no special provisions or specifications. Six aircraft, c/n 182 to c/n 187, became Mexican Air Force aircraft No. 1 through 6. They were delivered by air and then nothing was heard of them for years. They were reportedly used at Monterey and Mexico City and then they disappeared.

Some were reported sold to a dealer in Venezuela and one turned up being rebuilt by the MAF Squadron 203 Flying Club in Ensenada. It was c/n 184, Field No. 3 of the Mexican Air Force. Never registered in Mexico, it was then purchased by Joel McNeal, an American from San Diego. It was subsequently registered as N7828C. It is now in Illinois as NC17360, using the "N" number of a Ryan long since gone.

Honduras placed the second foreign order in May, 1938. These were to be armed single seat fighters with a single gun on the fuselage just forward of the cockpit, reminiscent of WW I fighters. They were delivered, however, with no guns mounted (just brackets and synchronizer) and the front pit covered over.

The overflight of Mexico was under the command of Capt. Malcolm Stewart. He and two Ryan employees, William Sloan and Harry Cameron, left San Diego June 13, 1937, after a fortnight's delay due to a revolution in Mexico. The flight was uneventful and slow because they were new aircraft.

On the leg from Tucson, Arizona, to El Paso, Texas, one incident did happen to Sloan. "I unfolded my map to study the territory ahead. I should have known better," he recalled, "than to attempt unraveling a section map in the cockpit. Suddenly soosh and overboard it went.

"I twisted frantically around and could see it plastered against my stabilizer, slowly showering the New Mexico landscape with piece after piece of map confetti. By almost standing on my head I could see the course line and read the landmarks. This unorthodox system continued for the next 40 or 50 miles until finally the whole map parted company with the stabilizer." He then flew south and picked up a railroad to El Paso.

"We headed across the flat Texas plains and about an hour out of Midland, enroute to San Antonio, we began to get into some scattered cumulus clouds. Their shade felt mighty good after the scorching sun of the previous day.

"Gradually, the clouds began to bunch together and formed an overcast at about 3,000 feet slowly lowering as we went on. With still 30 minutes to go we began dodging rain squalls. The ceiling dropped to 100 feet and visibility about a mile. We crowded together in a tight formation and went through. Randolph was the only field open and we glided in on the long turf runway with a sigh of relief."

None of the Honduran Ryans have survived.

BASSETT

Honduras Air Force No. 25 after crash at Comayagua

Col. James Bassett, owner of STM-2, Ryan N9761, c/n 452, a United States Air Force adviser to Honduras in 1974-75, tried to trace them and found only a Menasco engine. He wrote that he was able to put together the story of one Ryan, No. 25 Honduras Air Force, c/n 191.

Col. Bassett wrote, "As I understand the tale passed along second hand by an old head, the ship disappeared with an instructor and student aboard. A search failed to turn up any trace of the bird, and it was suspended. Some time later, a shopkeeper in Comayagua became suspicious of some Indians who were spending what seemed to him an inordinate amount of money for folks of their means.

"He reported it to the local fuzz, who leaned on the Indians, who owned up to removing said money from a couple of troops who had no further need of worldly goods. The Indians took the authorities to the site of the crash where the bodies were removed for burial. From the photos, it would appear that the Ryan hit from a flat spin, but that's merely conjecture on my part.

"The wreck was removed, according to two sources, and is part of the landfill upon which now sits the Air Force automotive repair shop. That much is a shame, for it would be quite a challenge to hunt down the wreck and snake it out if it were still there."

A letter from William P. (Doc) Sloan sheds light on another Ryan. He relates, "Malcolm (Mac) Stewart, 31, who was then Chief of the Honduranian Air Force, stayed on for a couple of years until his death in Tegucigalpa. He took off one morning from the airport there in one of the STMs. A wasp had built a nest in the air intake for the carburetor, and the nest was sucked into the engine, causing a sudden stoppage that resulted in Mac creaming the STM in the rocks in the canyon just beyond the airport. Mac survived, but was never quite right in the head, and ended up blowing out his brains sitting on a bar stool in a pub in Tegucigalpa a few months later."

Guatemala placed two orders for STM-1 aircraft, one on July 12, 1938, and the other on December 15, 1938. The first was for unarmed trainers, c/n 192 through 197. The second was for armed aircraft, c/n 300 through 305, with guns installed on the wings. The order also specified enough equipment and guns to arm the prior order of six. These were Colt 7mm machine guns and fired outboard of the propeller arc.

An interesting note on this second order is about the painting of the Guatemalan national insignia, which is similar in color and size to the early United States star except that it is six-pointed. The star was inadvertently painted using five-points.

RYAN

(Left) Second order of STM-1 aircraft for Guatemala with wing guns and incorrect star.

(Below) Guatemalan STM-1 trainers with correct star and no guns. Note the Ryan administration and school building in the background.

William Wagner shot a sequence of ground and air photos of the aircraft in this condition. This gave rise to the idea that the U.S. used them, which is not true. The star was repainted before delivery of the aircraft.

Seven Guatemalan Ryans survived and all are now complete, most still flying in the late '70s. The first two, c/n 302 and 304, were returned to St. Petersburg, Florida, in 1958 by Dick Spencer and Jerry McMullen. Spencer was flying cargo trips to Guatemala and brought the parts back in otherwise empty C-46 freighters. The STM aircraft returned were c/ns 193, 195, 197, 302, 303, and 304.

RYAN

Shortly afterwards, Sam Poole, a mechanic, was paid by the Guatemalans for his services in the form of aircraft parts. He was mostly interested in a Waco biplane but the "parts" included five Ryans. They were disassembled and little effort was used to mate them with their original engines, wings, and tails. This seems of little importance, but caused considerable difficulties in identifying these planes later on.

When Spencer and McMullen brought the STMs back, the FAA was reluctant to license them. If the officials involved had checked the blue prints or contacted the factory engineers instead of creating a wall of red tape, this problem would not have occurred.

Dick Spencer sold c/n 302 to Cotton Hodges who finally got it registered and licensed and then sold one-half share to Bill Dodd, who now owns the whole plane. Jerry McMullen had c/n 304 and after seeing the problem Dick had, sold his plane to Robert Webb, who also had trouble with the FAA. It was registered as N10535 and flew in Florida and Arkansas in the late 1950s and then disappeared.

Somewhere along the line, c/n 304 became c/n 173 and is currently in Illinois. John Lamb flew this STM in many exhibitions and air shows in the middle 1960s. After a short period of storage, it was sold to

John and Dave Dacy at Harvard, Illinois.

Lt. Col. Edward Ortowski obtained three complete Guatemalan Ryans and parts enough to almost make a fourth. He registered three of them using NC numbers from previously destroyed STAs. They are c/n 192, NC17350; c/n 193, NC17351; and c/n 195, NC17349.

He flew NC17349 from his home airfield, "The Eagles Nest," prior to his death in a duster accident. Number 193 was sold to King Eggar in Texas and the incomplete parts bearing Guatemalan AF field number 22 ended up at the San Diego Aerospace Museum.

The problem was that c/n 193 is field number 22 and now two aircraft claimed the same c/n. The fact is that Eggar owns c/n 193 and the Aerospace Museum has rebuilt the parts as a static display bearing the markings of the prototype ST c/n 101, NC14223.

Bolivia obtained a lend/lease agreement for Ryan airplanes during WW II. One was delivered in 1940, but it was a civilian STA, c/n 199, NC18905. The long delivery flight was made to Cochabamba airfield without any trouble. The first flight from Cochabamba ended in a severely damaged aircraft—probably because of the 7,000 foot altitude and the overweight General in the front cockpit. It was reported derelict, years later, in the Pan American Grace Hangar at Cochabamba. One known effort was made to locate it, but without success. (Note: It was found less than one mile from the airport and brought to the U. S. in the late 1970s.)

In 1938, the U. S. Army was interested in purchasing virtually any aircraft it could for cadet training. The Army tested an STA, c/n 306, and called it XPT-16. The aircraft was not exactly what the Army wanted, except it was readily available. The Air Corps preferred radial powered biplanes that were strong and with heavy controls like the fighters of the period. The little low wing Ryan was hand made, light, and forgiving at the controls, and had a Menasco engine which no other Army trainer had.

But in spite of this, 15 YPT-16 aircraft were ordered (16 were delivered) for a price of $96,275. All were supplied with hand crank direct drive Bendix starters and a military paint job. These planes became the first low wing primary trainers in the Air Corps inventory and were built under contract #PO-5607, specification #R 703-9.

Considerable redesign of the basic airframe was undertaken to try to conform to military specifications. The result was the model two airframe with its toe brakes, parking brake, larger cockpit openings, and the longeron outside the cockpit to make more room for the pilots. They also had adjustable seats and a canvas baggage hold on the back of the front seat.

Fortunately, the Ryan company added these changes to the civilian STC so they could be licensed as standard STA-2 aircraft. The Army ordered 30 of

PT-20A modification of earlier model with Kinner B5 engine of 125 hp. RYAN

Ethel Dodd and PT-20A, c/n 352, at Hayward Aviation about 1954. B. DODD

the more advanced design Ryans, again with Menasco engines. They were designated PT-20 and ordered under contract #AC-13316, specification #R-703-5 and priced at $6,380 each.

A third order for PT-20 aircraft was contract #AC-15566, specification #R-703-8, which called for 773 airplanes. This contract was amended to call for PT-21 and -22 airplanes.

A crash program was instigated to replace the Menasco engines which in hard Army use did not give good service. A possible alternative for the Menasco C4, 125 hp (L-365-1) inline powered ST resulted in the testing of Warner Super Scarab engines of 125 hp and 145 hp. Tests showed the combination to be excellent.

Unfortunately, the Warner engines were in such great demand that procurement in sufficient numbers was difficult. The Air Corps preference for radial engines and the readily available Kinner engines made them the logical choice.

The actual story of the two Ryan ST-2 aircraft is very confusing to say the least. The first aircraft, c/n 337, had the higher registration number X18920 and was the military configuration ST-2, while c/n 338, X18919, was an early type ST-1 airframe. Both aircraft were registered through 1944 in the U.S. Civil Registry as STWs. This last fact was simply an administrative oversight, as the tests took only a few short weeks.

At this point the histories of c/n 337 and c/n 338 become so involved that it would be best to quote a letter from William Wagner of the Ryan Aeronautical Company:

"On March 12, 1940, the Air Corps Training Detachment in San Diego accepted PT-20 manufacturer's c/n 337, equipped with a Menasco C4 engine. On November 20, 1940, the same Air Corps detachment accepted c/n 337 with modification to PT-20A, accomplished by installation of the Kinner B5 engine, R-440-1, in place of the Menasco C4. Number 337 had Air Corps #40-2401.

"Now we get into a fine discrepancy on c/n 338. The same acceptance form, the original of which I have, shows this plane with Air Corps serial #40-53 was delivered as a PT-20 on August 9, 1939. Going back to our PT-16 records I find that PT-16 with Air Corps #40-52 had manufacturer's c/n 320, while c/n 321 had Air Corps #40-54. Number 320 and 321 were delivered in October, 1939, and converted to PT-16A configuration in January, 1940. The fact that Air Corps #40-53 was skipped and later used for c/n 338 would lead me to believe, as is clear from the pictures, that this was an original PT-16 configuration, not a PT-20."

Official orders were signed by Brig. Gen. K. B. Wolf to approve the engine change. Fourteen PT-16s were converted between January and April, 1941, to PT-16A configuration with Kinner B5, 125 hp engines. Twenty seven PT-20s were converted to PT-20A configuration from March to October, 1940. It is to be noted that two PT-20 aircraft were experimentally converted to Menasco D4 engines in January and March, 1941, making the model PT-20B. These were then converted a second time to PT-20A.

Unfortunately, Washington procurement officers later refused to pay for the cost incurred in converting these 41 trainers. This resulted in a trip to Washington where Claude Ryan took up the problem with his old friend General Henry "Hap" Arnold who quickly ended the crisis and payment was made.

The flying record of the PT-16 and PT-20 aircraft was surprisingly good. The 46 aircraft flew 44,025 hours in military service before being wrecked or declared surplus (class 26). This averages out to be 957 hours per plane with the low time of 188 hours (c/n 342) to a high of 1,342 (c/n 329). The average length of time in service was only 29 months.

Although the safety record was enviable, the time per aircraft per day flying was poor. The first ten months at San Diego saw 10,000 accident free hours of instruction, which projects out to about one million miles of safe flying. The PT-22 did much better per day and with a great deal higher utilization prior to being sold or wrecked. The safety record at Hemet and Tucson for PT-22s was very good, but the PT-21s at King City did not fare well at all, with 65 accidents and five fatalities in 18 months. Bear in mind that Hemet and Tucson were Ryan Schools and King City was not.

The late forties and fifties saw few of these planes on the suprlus market; the only one on the Civil Air Registry was N69094, a PT-20A, and still carrying the original Kinner engine in the late '50s.

In the early 1970s, a PT-20A was discovered at a trade school in Oakland, California. How it came to be there is not known. The key to its obscurity was the Kinner engine. Many people passed it by simply because they thought it was a PT-22. The ship was bought by Don Carter of California.

Don and Fred Sorenson found another PT-20 in a Los Angeles A&P school being used as a taxi trainer without wings. It had field number 57 still painted on its side, but no other identification. This Ryan is once again equpiped with a Menasco engine, and is flying under an old STM registration.

The Republic of China order dated November 15, 1939, called for 50 Ryan STM-2 military land plane trainers. Although these model designations were not

Central Aviation Manufacturing Co. hangar at Loiwing, China in 1941 after bombing raid by Japanese. Two burnt out Ryans are left. GERRY BEAUCHAMP

Captured Dutch Army Ryan, Java, 1941. J. L. CASIUS

subsequently used, the agreement called for 48 STC-4 primary two-place trainers and 2 STC-P4 single place pursuit trainers. The power plant specified for both models was the 155 hp Menasco C4S-2. The pursuit trainers were to have, as standard equipment, one 30 caliber fixed machine gun installed inside the fuselage.

The contract was negotiated through China Airmotive Company and included manufacturing rights by the Central Aircraft Manufacturing Co. of Loiwing, China. These rights were never used. All planes shipped from San Diego were model STM-2E, c/n 356-374, 377-405 and 406, and STM-2P, c/n 375 and 376. The first shipment was made in February, 1940 and the last planes arrived in China in the spring of 1941.

Six Ryan STM aircraft were known to have been lost at Loiwing in a Japanese bombing attack. Twenty Ryans were at Kunming late in 1941 and about half were destroyed or damaged.

Kunming was a major Flying Tiger base (AVG) and George J. Brice was stationed there as the assistant maintenance chief, from January, 1942, to December, 1942. While the 2nd Pursuit AVG was at Kunming he saw the Ryans parked in earth-work revetments and not used at all by the Chinese.

During off hours, the American maintenance personnel would repair and fly them for sport. The Chinese would allow this for a time, and then retrieve the plane only to have it replaced with another inoperative ship until most were in flying condition.

When the 2nd Pursuit left Kunming, 12 Ryans were in serviceable condition. None were damaged by the AVG personnel at this base and none were damaged by enemy action. Still the Chinese would not use them. There is no report of any armed Ryans in this group of planes.

One of the twelve Ryans from Kunming was used by the 75th Squadron USAF at Than Yi until about July, 1942. Major Tex Hill, formerly of the AVG, commanded this unit and Capt. John R. Allison was one of the pilots. It was Capt. Allison (Maj. Gen., USAF, retired) that related this tale about one of the Ryans.

"Kunming was only 50 miles away and a pleasant flight in an open cockpit plane. Hill and Allison had checked themselves out in the Ryan and it was a welcome diversion from the usual P-40. A daily mail run was flown to Kunming, almost always by a Lt. Elwood Kluks. He was a good, but reckless, pilot who had survived combat flying and a crash landing.

"On this particular day, a passenger had made the trip to Kunming and Kluks flew back alone with the mail in a musitte bag strapped to the front seat. He had a rather complex routine upon returning home. On the down-wind leg over the runway he would roll inverted and glide the length of the field and then split S in for a landing. With the event of the silent engine, which would quit inverted, the Squadron personnel would know Kluks was home with the mail.

"In the last flight the musitte bag had been improperly secured and had dropped down between the stick and the front seat. This prevented the stick from being pulled back but did not stop the plane from rolling inverted. The plane dove straight into the ground, killing Lt. Kluks."

One of the flight schools that used the Ryans was located at Poashan, which is southeast of Kunming. The commanding officer of this small Chinese field was Capt. Konsin Shah. When he was contacted in 1977 he had become Consul General Shah (Republic of China, New York). He spoke of only one unusual incident involving Ryan trainers.

"One day in the early afternoon, a critique was held of the morning's flying. The school was expecting a group of new Ryans to augment the six already on the field. The students were gathered around the instructor, away from the aircraft, and under a tree when a student said, 'Here come the new Ryans.'

"The planes could be heard and seen approaching and they were nearly overhead when it was realized that they were Japanese fighter bombers! There are a number of Japanese low-wing monoplanes with fixed landing gear and big wheel pants that loosely resemble the Ryan. The Japanese bombed and strafed the field destroying some planes and damaging others. None of those hit were the Ryans."

When asked about other stories he said, "What can you say about a trainer? It did its job well and that is about all there is to it."

The Chinese did order some PT-22 trainers, but there is very little evidence that many ever left India on their way to China. Col. Robert L. Scott (AVG) makes a reference to a Ryan trainer being transported in a DC-3 over the Hump to China in his book, *God is my Co-pilot.* Capt. Allison is reported as seeing one in an old monastery. Another, that could have been an STM, was spotted in a cave with other arms stored for use at a later date, presumably against the Communists.

A recent letter written to the Republic of China asking about information on these planes was answered by General Wu Yueh. The letterhead revealed him as the Commanding General of the Chinese Air Force. He included a picture of a PT-22 in Chinese markings and stated that it was used by the Chinese Air Force Academy. Unfortunately, there was no date given and the location of the picture was not identified.

The last that was seen of any Chinese Ryans was at Hong Kong in 1950. The revolution was over and a large number of Nationalist aircraft, including two STMs that had been flown there to escape the Communists, were impounded by the British. One fact remains. Three Australian Ryans were shipped to Hong Kong about this time, and it is known that four left the city. The last was an unidentified, incomplete machine that had been used by an A&P school and laid out in back of a hangar for years. All *four* ultimately returned to America.

Captured Chinese Ryan with Japanese pilots in 1942. Photo from a Japanese newspaper. J. L. CASIUS

Chapter Three

ST-3KB, prototype ST-3, NX18925, with a Kinner B54, 125 hp engine. RYAN

Sport Trainer Model-3 (ST-3)

Ryan ST-3KB was the first prototype built on October 9, 1940. It carried c/n 1000, NX18925, and was never a military aircraft, but remained at the factory for test purposes. Powered by a 125 hp Kinner B-54 engine, it had landing gear covers but no fairings on the wheels themselves. This model was never issued a civilian ATC. The design was intended as a mass production replacement for the earlier hand-made sport planes. They incorporated heavy aircraft characteristics and changes brought about by military experience in Primary Training operations.

Ryan ST-3KR, a second prototype, was c/n 1001, NX18926, the forerunner of the PT-21, PT-22 and NR-1 aircraft. It was used by the military for in-service tests, but was never officially an Army aircraft. While carrying a Kinner R-55 or R-56 engine it conformed with specifications for the civilian ATC 749, issued February 16, 1942. This particular aircraft was still flying as late as 1976 as an ST-3KR with an R-56 Kinner. It is one of the finest examples of a well kept and beautiful Ryan

The above airplane was the prototype of the PT-21 series, c/n #1001, NC18926. The airplane was tested at Wright Field in Ohio. It still had the civilian markings. The airplane in the photo has a Kinner R-52, however, the production PT-21s all had Kinner R-440-3, 132 hp engines. The airplane was registered in California in 1975 with a Kinner R-56 engine.

anywhere, and even sports the original type landing gear fairings.

Ryan ST-3M was a model that was ordered by the Dutch on May 26, 1941. They were to be powered by the 160 hp Menasco D-4B engines. The order was amended and then cancelled. No ST-3 aircraft were built with Menasco engines.

Ryan ST-3S prototytpe was NX18925, fitted with twin Edo floats. Three aircraft were delivered and all went to Ecuador on lend/lease (c/n 1078-1080 AF s/n 41-15174-15176). The Dutch order for 25 was cancelled and were ultimately delivered to the U.S. Army as PT-22A on wheels.

Three major experiments were carried out using NX18925 — the original ST-3KB. None were given model designations, but all were important and should be given recognition. The "Canadian enclosure," or hatch cover for the normally open cockpits, was an attempt to sell enclosed aircraft to Canada for winter operations. Only a test canopy and not the complete model was ever produced. A "speed ring" was added for possible cooling and air speed benefits. One was tested and none were used on production aircraft. The Lycoming engine, Model O-435, was also tested on NX18925. Very good results were obtained, which is possibly the reason it was installed as standard equipment on the later YPT-25.

Ryan PT-21 was the first Army designation for the ST-3. Army Air Corps contract AC-15566, specificiation R-703-10, called for 775 airplanes. These were delivered as 100 PT-21s, 100 NR-1s, and 575 PT-22s. This is the same order with a different specification dash number under which 773 PT-20 aircraft were ordered and then cancelled.

Experimental "Canadian enclosure" on NX18925 and not used on any production models. RYAN

Basically the airframe for all PT-21, PT-22 and NR-1 aircraft remained the same throughout production. The differences were in the engines, aileron counterbalance arms and paint trim. The hundred PT-21 aircraft were manufactured in 1941 using 132 Kinner R-440-3 engines (c/n 1002-1059, 1061-

RYAN

RYAN

(Above) Experimental "Speedring" on NX18925 was not used on production models.

(Left) ST-3S seaplane prototype NX18925. Three were built and sold to Ecuador.

1076, 1155-1180). Most were converted to PT-22 configuration by removing the landing gear fairings, changing the aileron counterbalance arms from the bottom to the top of the wing and installing a 160 hp Kinner R-540-1 engine, (civilian nomenclature, R-55). All had unpainted fuselages with yellow wings and tails. Most were used at the Army contract school at Palo Alto Field, King City, California.

Ryan NR-1s were built alongside the PT-21 as the Navy counterpart. They were identical to the Army model except for a lockable tail wheel controllable from the cockpit and the paint trim. Of the hundred built (c/n 1060, 1081-1154, 1181-1205), the Navy used 99 at Jacksonville, Florida Naval Air Station and one at Kopper's Company in Lancaster, Pennsylvania. Only three are known to have been sold surplus— c/n 1129, N66622; c/n 1200, N31687; and c/n not known, N67640. NR-1 aircraft were delivered with unpainted fuselage and yellow tail. The landing gear fairings were mostly removed in service.

Ryan PT-22 Recruit (PT-22C), was the most common variant with 1,023 being delivered with Kinner R-540-1. The government paid $8,473 for each, which in comparison with the price paid for other primary trainers, was a bargain. They are identical to prior models except the aileron counterbalance arms are on top and there were no landing gear fairings. Seventy were ordered by the Republic of China, but it is believed only a few reached their destination. Two hundred and fifty were converted to Kinner R-540-3 engines (civilian nomenclature, R-56) and became PT-22C models. There was no PT-22B model, either by manufacturer's designation or conversion.

Ryan PT-22A was a designation applied because they were fitted with provisions for twin floats. They were originally ordered by the Netherlands Purchasing Commission on May 26, 1941 (see Model ST-3S). The order was amended January 8, 1942, and called for 25 seaplanes, equipped with Kinner R-55 engines. In the meantime Java fell to the Japanese and the aircraft (order number PNR #N-463) were to be delivered to the Dutch Flying School at Jackson, Mississippi.

Fifty-five primary trainers were needed at this school and it was decided that since only the Western Training Command was using the Ryans, the PT-19

PT-22 Standard configuration production model. RYAN

was to be standard equipment of the South East Training Command. To everyone's surprise the 25 ST-3s in Dutch markings were flown into Jackson AFB in May, 1942, by a group of ferrying pilots. It turned out that some unknown party had goofed and not cancelled the order for the delivery to Jackson. The whole group was turned back and returned to California for subsequent sale to the U. S. Army.

The PT-22 was well built and strong, the same as the fighters of the period. These and other Ryans trained 14,000 pilots for the Army and Navy during the war. The bulk of this service was in PT-21 and PT-22 aircraft.

Out of the thousands of stories told over the years, a few are related here for an insight into the airplanes, instructors and the wartime Primary Training Program.

Instructor Bill Sloan tells of a situation at Rosedale, an auxiliary field outside of San Diego. "Rosedale was located on a piece of rolling real estate that had quite a hump in the middle. We'd land uphill bounce over the crest, and brake to a rolling stop on the downhill side. Watching a solo student land from the head of the runway was always an experience. The Stearman biplanes weren't quite as suspenseful as the Ryan PTs because when a student ground looped on the downhill side with the biplane, we could watch the upper wing rotating. In the Ryans we could only watch the cloud of dust and wonder what in the hell was happening."

Clarence Prescott, also a Ryan instructor, was having a hard time with an inept student. "There's nothing like a hard rap in the belly to get a student's undivided attention," Sloan said, "and this could be accomplished by pushing the stick forward and then yanking it back. Watching his student very carefully in the rear-view mirror, Clarence suffered through the second climbing turn at 400 feet and then whopped the stick forward, diving the plane. The student had forgotten to fasten his seat belt, and he popped out of the cockpit like a pea from a pod, still in a sitting position with his hands where they should have been on the stick and throttle, but actually about 5 feet above the airplane. Fortunately, the student popped his chute in time, and it blossomed just before he hit the ground. No injuries, but we all learned a lesson."

The fact that more than half of PT-22 aircraft survived the war and that over 250 were still registered by 1964, with 120 licensed that year, is a great tribute to the people at Ryan Aeronautical. These numbers are down to 172 registered and 81 licensed for 1982. One enigma that remains without an answer is why many were purchased surplus and registered, but never licensed. These are not isolated cases, for there are groups of up to ten and twelve airplanes, bought by different individuals, that were registered and never heard of again.

On the surplus market, the price ranged from a low of $600 to about $1,000. By 1965 the price started up sharply and good flying planes went for $1,800 and up. Today this price is in the $24,000 range and still going up. It should not be really surprising, but the average condition is generally much better now than 20 years ago. No longer do you see one tied down, forgotten and forlorn. The days are gone when any PT-22 is junked; even when wrecked, the parts are sold for an ever increasing price.

In the last 35 years, these ships have been built up from parts so many times that it is hard to keep track of them, particularly with the constant changes of "N" numbers and paint jobs. As late as 1971, two PT-22s were found in a shed in Vidor, Texas, and bought for $500. The first, c/n 1604, N59466, was rebuilt and flying in one year. The other, c/n 1809, N54004, went to California. The point is that these planes can still be had for a reasonable price — if you look hard and long enough.

One aircraft, N487H, was lost due to arson. It was painted in pseudo Army colors and locked in a hangar near Milwaukee. The fire was deliberately set in the cockpit by someone who presumably did not like the military.

Four PT-22s are now in museums. Three of these are flying with the Confederate Air Force, including c/n 2248, N883D, which was the last ST-3 built.

N51122, c/n 2204, was used in the 1974 TV show, *M*A*S*H.* It was painted with Chinese markings and equipped with wooden "bombs." Unfortunately, the credibility and capabilities of everything and everybody in the episode were strained beyond belief.

My first Ryan was a PT-22, (c/n 1371, AF 41-15342) registered as N46504. All her Army records were still intact and her field number was 346. The flying hours were 3,200 of cadet and civilian use, with only one accident involving a broken propeller. She had a total of six different engines and three fabric jobs.

One long afternoon, I flew her more than 400 miles with no hint of trouble. The next day, the engine, with only 350 hours since new, would not turn over. The propeller was free to turn a few degrees and then it would jam. The R-55 was torn down to find a broken master rod knuckle pin which was catching on the fly weight. It had been broken a long time and the assembly was ruined. Back in those days, a new R-56 Kinner could be bought for $500, and we were flying again in a week.

In the summer of 1965 we took off from Waukegan, Illinois, and then flew out over Lake Michigan heading northeast for 50 miles. Then the Ryan was turned north and this course was held for 30 minutes. We were equipped with a Bayside radio and were in contact with Milwaukee Flight Service. Before takeoff, we had spoken by radio phone to the captain of the Christian Radich, a square rigged ship on her way to visit Chicago. I had never seen a full rigged ship and thought if anything might rival the beauty of a Ryan, it would have to be a square rigged ship under sail! We found her, buzzed her and photographed her.

N56504 flew on for two more years and a total time of 3,652 hours and was destroyed in a fatal accident August, 1967. The pilot at the time of the crash was seen to make a turn at 1,200 feet and stall, then spin, recover and spin again in the other direction, before hitting the ground flat in a high speed stall.

This pilot did everything wrong; in no way was the PT-22 at fault. She had recovered in plenty of time, but because of an inept pilot it was the end. (The point is, we have a good plane here that flew all those hours safely, which nobody remembers, and then is wrecked in a fatal crash which is the only part ever brought to mind.)

Another, not quite as violent, example is the end of c/n 1608, N25510, on January 8, 1968. She was flown to Ottumwa the previous year, a really nice old aircraft. In the winter, after being purchased by an airline pilot, the ferry flight was started late in the afternoon. A short time later, it was dark and the pilot was lost. He made an approach for an off field landing, but failed to see some power lines. The Ryan was totally smashed, but the pilot was, fortunately, unhurt.

There was a story about the individual who showed up for the National Aerobatic Contest at one of the early Reno Air Races in a PT-22. With the pilot weighing about 300 pounds and a field elevation of 5,000 feet, this guy was in trouble before he even began. He was doing pretty well until he lost her in a maneuver, recovering just as he was dusting the sage brush. This apparently scared the fellow so badly that he immediately landed and was not heard from again.

According to Bill Richards, a current PT-22 owner, a gaggle of Northern California Ryans departed Paso Robles heading home, on the last day of the 1973 West Coast Ryan Fly-In. As usual, various planes were alternately flying formation or dog fighting as the group made its way up the Solinas Valley.

Two of the aircraft, an STM and a PT-22 were playing follow the leader and were steaming full throttle up a dry stream bed at 20 feet altitude. Suddenly the STM, which was leading, did a near vertical pull-up much to the suprise of the PT-22 driver who, too late, saw a single telephone wire stretched across the stream bed. A slight jolt and the PT was still flying with a shaken pilot. A quick inspection by the other plane revealed no visible damage or trailing wire and, as the Kinner was still running well, the much subdued pilot proceeded home at a considerably more respectable altitude.

Two incidents one year apart took place at the Sackettville Airport, home to many of California's San Francisco and Marian County antiquers. The first involved a PT-22 owner who had just finished a rebuild of his plane the previous winter. For some reason the plane seemed to have accumulated some dust or debris inside the fuselage. On the second or third touch-and-go landing that first day of flight testing, the pilot, with his goggles shoved up on his helmet, suddenly was temporarily blinded by dust blowing into his eyes. When he could see again, he was too low and too short. He applied full power, but too late, and the plane settled in, hitting the ditch at the runway threshold. Over she went, totaling herself. In the best PT-22 tradition, however, the cockpit section stayed relatively intact and the pilot got away with only a few injuries.

A year later another PT-22 was being flight tested after a beautiful and complete rebuild. Again on the second or third landing the pilot was floating the plane on with full flaps at an altitude of 15-20 feet when the flap rachet slipped. The plane settled and hit so hard it broke the fuselage aft of the cockpit and ruined the stub wings.

Ryan flaps were considered so untrustworthy that at the WW II primary flight schools the instructors would have the students go through the motions of pumping down the flaps, but the flaps themselves were not used.

It was June, 1975, and the first day of the annual West Coast Ryan Fly-In. Twenty planes had arrived at Paso Robles and the pilots, copilots, wives, girlfriends and ground crews all hangar flying when a gentleman showed up nearly speechless with excitement.

He had been driving up U.S. 101 heading north and had just come to Paso Robles. He could scarcely believe his ears when he heard the radio say that there would be a gathering of Ryans at the local airport that weekend. He had been a flight instructor at King City, California, during WW II, teaching in Ryans and was headed for a reunion of King City and Dos Palos flight instructors, held every ten years. Arrangements were made for a contingent of Ryans to make a fly-by on their way home and then land for a few hours of story telling and flying.

Only a few years before, an average of 12 PT-22 trainers would show up at Ottumwa, Iowa, for the National Fly-In. There were 14 Ryans of all types in a fly-by in 1967. This is no longer the case, as only three or four now attend each year. The center of Ryan activities, particularly with the PT-22s, has definitely shifted to California.

One last note. Although ST-3 aircraft were STC'd for civilian use, none were ordered by civilians. They were also never amended on their certificate for floats or skis.

STK, experimental test aircraft for Kinner engines on Ryan ST-1 and ST-2 airframes. Shown is NX18924, c/n 406. Note: late military windshields. RYAN

RYAN ST3-S SEAPLANE

SKETCHES BY BUD STONE

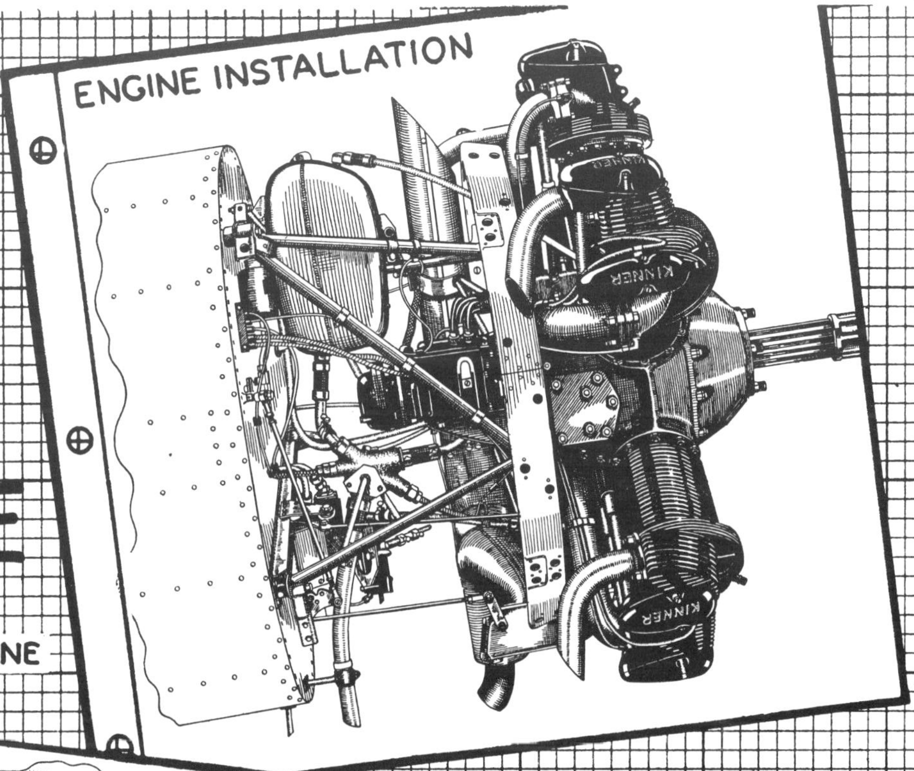

ENGINE INSTALLATION

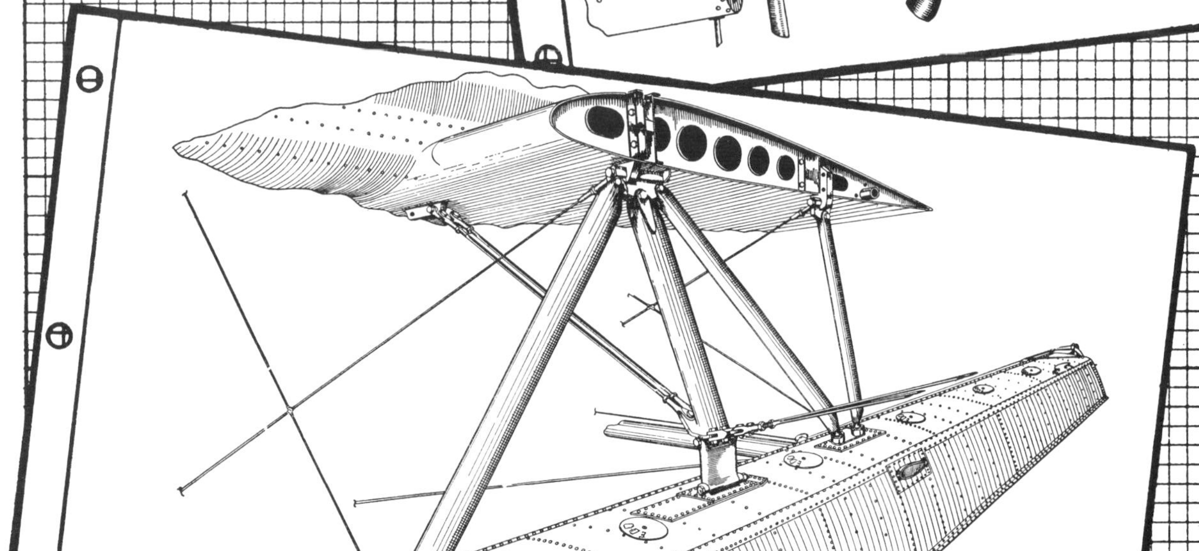

SEAPLANE GEAR

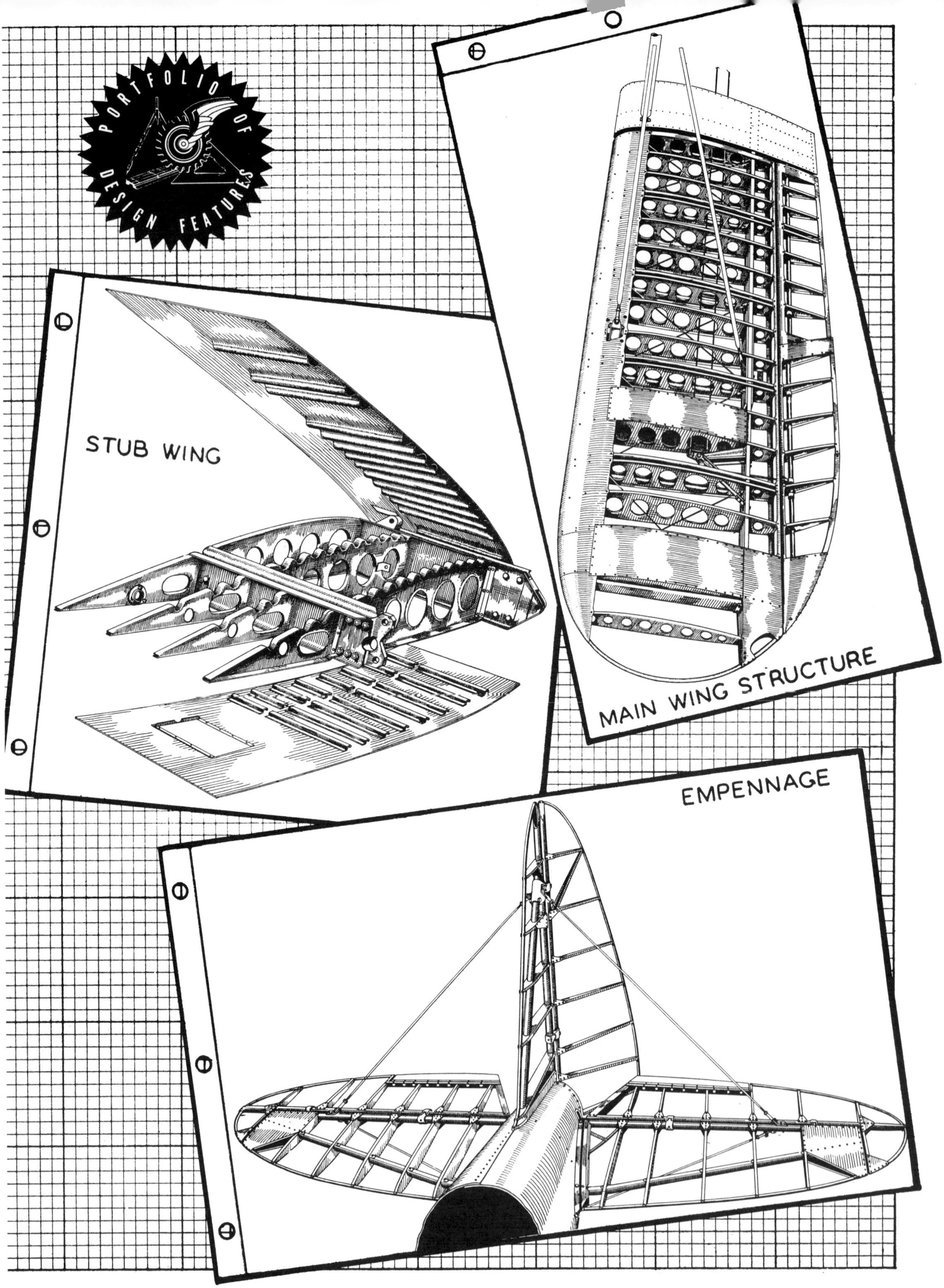
PORTFOLIO OF DESIGN FEATURES
STUB WING
MAIN WING STRUCTURE
EMPENNAGE

Chapter Four

YPT-25, Ryan ST-4. Only five test aircraft were built. U.S. AIR FORCE

Sport Trainer Model-4 (ST-4) (YPT-25)

Five experimental Air Corps Trainers were built on contract AC-21204, specification 714-2, which called for a minimum of strategic materials. They were powered by a 185 hp opposed Lycoming 0-435-1, and were completely built of bonded plywood with the exception of the engine, gear and cowl. This was the first and only Ryan capable of front seat solo in the Sport Trainer series. They were equipped for blind and night flying training. Like some other Ryan experimentals, they were good planes, but developed too late in the war and never reached the mass production stage. There is no record of service after they were flown away from San Diego by the WASPs. YPT-25, s/n 42-8703, was surveyed at Salina, Kansas Sept. 2, 1943 and s/n 42-8705 was surveyed at Cimmarron Field, Sept. 13, 1944. As for the other airplanes (42-8704, 42-8706 and 42-8707), there is no data.

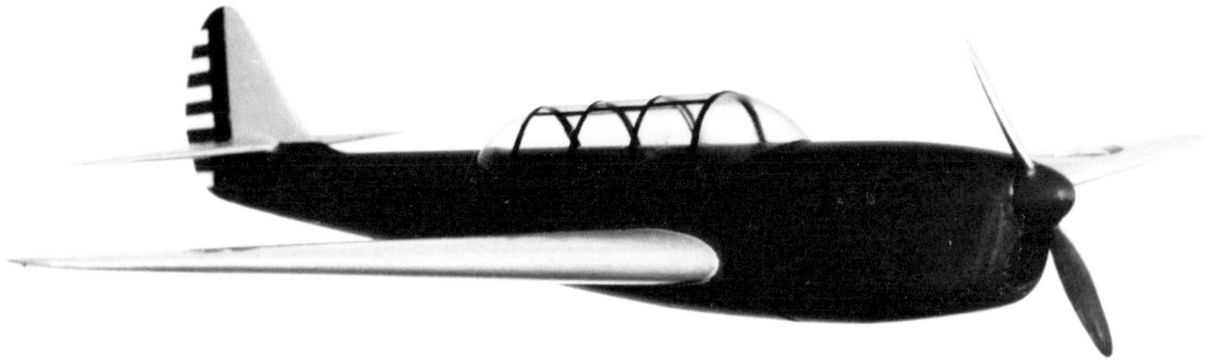

Proposed Ryan Basic Trainer, conventional tail model. RYAN

Proposed Ryan Basic Trainer of 1939, twin tail variant. RYAN

Ryan Basic Trainer

This Ryan Basic Trainer was proposed to the Army Air Corps in a report dated September 30, 1939. It would have been in the Sport Trainer series had it been built. However, two models of the trainer were built, one with conventional tail and the other with twin vertical stabilizers and rudders. Both designs called for retractable conventional landing gear. Not much data is known and because it never proceeded beyond the model and planning stage, only estimated performance figures are available:

Speed	205 mph at sea level
Engine	Ranger V-820C-1 of 375 hp
Gross weight	3,400 lbs.
Range	688 miles at 162 mph
Absolute ceiling	26,000 ft.

Chapter Five

RYAN

Ryan Schools

The Ryan Flying Company operated three rebuilt Standards mostly for sightseeing, with a little flight instruction in Jennys and a regular Sunday afternoon exhibition in a Thomas-Morse Scout. This was 1924 when the first unincorporated school, airline and flying business was operated out of the Dutch Flats airfield in San Diego. T. C. Ryan acquired a partner — B. Franklin Mahoney.

The young company continued to grow and entered the manufacturing of aircraft field with the M-1. A photograph taken in 1926 shows the hangar painted, "Ryan Flying Co." and "School of Aviation." The flying students in some cases paid for flying lessons by working in the factory. During this period the "school" had on-the-job training for skills such as welders.

On November 29, 1926, the partnership was dissolved, and on May 1, 1928, Ryan was back in business at Dutch Flats — this time as the "Ryan Flying School." Now it really *was* a school, not just haphazard instruction. An actual curriculum of flight training, day and night, instruments, and cross-country training, were required before graduation. The Department of Commerce rated this school very highly, and awarded it one of four certificates in the country for training Transport pilots.

By 1929, Ryan Airport at Dutch Flats had become the commercial flying center of the Southwest. Ryan again changed the company name, this time to "T. C. Ryan Flying School." The firm name was again changed January 5, 1931, to "The Ryan School of Aeronautics, Ltd.," and incorporated for the first time.

In spite of the Depression, they operated two Wacos, a DH Moth, several Jennys, some Standards, and one M-2. The next major change came in the form of standardizing most of the trainers. The choice of the Great Lakes, powered by the Cirrus engine with Ryan as the California distributor, gave the program a more diversified appeal.

In 1932, after Lindbergh Field was built, Ryan moved his operation into a new terminal building he had to build himself. The next year, the Cleveland firm building Great Lakes folded. The training now offered included flight, welding, sheet metal work, and aeronautical engineering.

1934 saw the first of the "New Ryan" ST trainers on the line. They were sleek and beautiful ships, drawing a great deal of attention to the school. Training was also offered in package deals, one price covering the aircraft and flight phase.

By 1938, enrollment had increased to over 100 students, and doubled again by 1939. Ryan was one of the nine civilian schools chosen by the Army to train Primary Cadets. Ryan was still at Lindbergh Field with approximately 200 students which accounted for 75 Army flying cadets, 25 commercial flight students, 25 aeronautical engineers and 90 mechanic students.

The Army course lasted three months and consisted of intensive instruction under Air Corps supervision, including 65 hours of flying and 225 hours of ground school. All the instructors were civilian, and the check pilot was Army. Lindbergh Field was not the best place for training of this sort because the training planes had no radio and the field was used by large military aircraft and civilian airline planes.

The Ryan School suspended its Lindbergh Field operations at the request of the military because San Diego, being on the coast, was declared a "combat zone" after Pearl Harbor. It moved its Army training to Hemet, California, and Tucson, Arizona. At this time it ceased teaching commercial pilots, aircraft mechanics, and engineers. The Ryan Aeronautical Institute continued to expand its home study instruction in aeronautical drafting, engineering, and aircraft maintenance.

With administrative headquarters in San Diego, Ryan operated three of the most efficient contract flying schools. Flight hours per plane had risen from an old average of 4 1/2 hours to 7 1/2 hours per day. Many new features were instituted, including parallel runways, whereby solo planes took off and turned left, while dual planes took off and turned right. The old practice of reserving specific planes for ranking officers was discontinued, women mechanics were used, and planes were fueled on the line by tank trucks.

A number of other schools used Ryan aircraft in the training of Army cadets, but they were not affiliated with Ryan. Two of the largest were King City, California, Palo Alto Field, and the Morton Air Academy at Blyth, California.

Many small operators also used Ryans. An example would be Tufts Edgcumbe at Palwaukee, Illinois. They contracted three classes of Naval Officers for flight training. These civilian contract schools are not to be confused with the Civilian Pilot Training Program; they are not synonymous.

When the Army training came to an end, the Ryan School ceased all operations and never resumed civilian training.

Ryan PT-22s, Ryan Field, Hemet, California, 1943.

RYAN

Ryan School of Aeronautics Chief Instructor Paul "Pablo" Wilcox at San Diego, 1937.

RYAN

Student (later instructor) Bill Evans and Chief Instructor Paul Wilcox with Ryan School STA, NC17359.

RYAN

The men who made the Ryan contract schools work, left to right, Paul Wilcox, T. C. Ryan, Capt. John C. Horton, Lt. Lloyd P. Hopwood, Earl Prudden and Walter K. Balk.

Instructor, student, and Ryan PT-22 at the Ryan School at Hemet. RYAN

Ryan PT-22 aircraft at Hemet, California, 1942. RYAN

Ryan Field, Hemet, California, 1943.

RYAN

Army "Dodo" walking punishment tour at the Ryan School at Hemet, California.

RYAN

PT-16 and PT-20, Ryan aircraft at San Diego, 1940. RYAN

PT-16A and PT-20A and students at the Ryan School in San Diego, 1941. RYAN

Chapter Six

Modified Ryans

Many Ryans have been modified at one time or another, but most were restored at a later date to original configuration. It is hard to understand how anyone with no training in aeronautical engineering can take a fine old antique airplane and modify it. These aircraft were designed by competent engineers and built in a factory under government supervision and test flown by expert pilots. Then, years later, one man takes it upon himself to make major changes. It is impossible to be competent in all three areas. The result is usually an unsaleable aircraft with lines and beauty ruined, the insurance rates increase, and the utility cut down.

There are exceptions to this, an example might be N42X. A Ranger engine with an Aeromatic propeller and long ailerons were installed in an STA by Bob Heuer. The work was completed by the owner, who was an expert pilot and an A&P mechanic. The date was September, 1967, before the complete dominance of aerobatics by the homebuilt biplane.

This Ryan was flown in unlimited competition in Monroe, Louisiana in 1968 and placed second. It was again flown by the owner's son, Mike, placing first in the primary class. In the next two years it flew at the EAA competition, placed second and won at the Dacy Fly-In in 1969. It no longer wins even though her next owner, John Gosney, is a good pilot. It has been for sale a number of years. Even with all these modifications, it is still unable to perform climbing maneuvers well, and the rate of roll is far too slow.

CARPENTER

Bob Heuer and modified STA, N42X, with Ranger engine.

The most bizarre modification of a Ryan was made to an ST-3, N47081. It was made into a biplane with a 220 hp Continental engine by Paul Eddy. The fuselage was shortened 14 1/2 inches because of the added engine weight and the front cockpit was eliminated. The wings were unique in that they retained the original stub wings and landing gear. The upper panels and the outer lower wings were level, creating an inverted gull wing effect with the stub wings which were not changed from their 4° dihedral. The new aircraft had a wing span of 25 ft., weight of 1,580 lbs. and cruised at 110 mph.

In the case of this plane, the owner spent a great deal of money, added 60 hp, lost the front cockpit, lost 60 miles in cruising range, gained 5 mph in cruising speed and went to an experimental license.

It was built primarily for exhibition work, and was sold to movie stunt man Cliff Winters. Winters used it in air shows, and performed generally in a very professional manner. These were low level exhibitions and, unfortunately, the plane crashed and the showman lost his life.

Painting most of these old planes, even though they were originally polished, is almost a necessity. Very little Alclad finish remains, and will no longer polish to a bright shine.

The STM aircraft in Australia have a number of modifications, three of which are required by the Department of Civil Aviation (DCA). The most noticeable is the reinforced lug for the landing gear wires on bulkhead #2, and the heavy stringers between #2 and #3 bulkheads on the outside of the belly. Also a repair of magneto switches are mounted on the outside of the fuselage near the crank starter. These switches are

N47081, c/n 1644, biplane with Cont. 220. BURTON KEMP

very handy, particularly if the plane is on floats or when the crank starter is used.

One civilian STA and at least three STMs were converted to DH 145 hp Gipsy engine power. This conversion carries an Australian STC and is well engineered. The plane looks the same, except that the propeller turns in the opposite direction and the exhaust stacks and pressure cowls are reversed.

Another Australian Ryan, No. 465, carries a Lycoming O-032A. The revised cowling completely spoiled the original classic lines and there was no improvement in performance. This small four cylinder 150 hp engine was used because the DCA would not allow use of an engine with more horsepower than the original. Converted originally for air show work, it had a smoke generating system and a Bayside radio. The conversion was very expensive, costing almost as much as the original cost of the airplane. It was for sale for over four years proving to be a very hard aircraft to sell. It has been reconverted to a C4S.

STA-Spl, NC17352, was used by Barnstorming Barnhills, Inc., during the 1950s and early '60s very successfully for air show work, using a Menasco C4S engine. After being sold, it was equipped with a Lycoming O-360 engine and a metal propeller. Although it flew well, it appears the modifications greatly compromised its looks. When the time came to sell it, it proved to be impossible. After being on the market over a year, it was re-equipped with the Menasco as part of the sales agreement and went to a California buyer.

John Gosney and modified STA, c/n 156, N17352. CARPENTER

(Above) STM, PI-X324, c/n 494 with Lyc O-435 engine. She is now in America flying as N14911 with a Menasco engine.

(Right) John Bang and Gipsy powered STM, c/n 467. Note spreader bar between landing gear.

(Below Left) Sherry's Speedster, c/n 2056, N60155 with Cont. W-670.

(Below Right) John Heller and PT-22A, c/n 1277, N58729. Tacoma, Wash.

CARPENTER

BURTON KEMP

BILL HODGES

Modified PT-22, N47082, c/n 1443 with Ranger engine. BURTON KEMP

Bob Yate's modified NR-1, N66622, c/n 1129 with Ranger engine.

Chapter Seven

Operational Dutch Army Ryans on Java 1941. CARPENTER

Netherlands Ryans

Five separate contracts for Ryan STM-E2 landplanes and STM-S2 seaplane trainers all to be equipped with Menasco C4S-2 supercharged 155 hp engines, were negotiated by the Netherlands East Indies Government during a five month period in 1940.

20 June 1940 - 40 STM-E2 landplane trainers

25 June 1940 - 12 STM-E2 landplane trainers and
- 12 pairs of Edo floats, model 1965

8 July 1940 - 12 STM-S2 seaplane trainers and
- 12 sets of landplane gears

15 August 1940 - 12 STM-E2 landplane trainers
- 12 STM-S2 seaplane trainers

7 October 1940 - 20 STM-E2 landplane trainers

Summary:
Total orders, original equipment, were:

84 STM-E2 landplane trainers
24 STM-S2 seaplane trainer
——
108 total

The floats were completed with water rudders which could be retracted and steered from the cockpit. On examination of the actual aircraft, it has been found that all were model STM-S2 regardless of the order specifications.

A Ryan advertisement giving the particulars for these seaplanes, printed in 1940, offered the following:

Extra Equipment - Rate of climb and turn and bank indicators; Machine gun synchronizing gears for engine; Machine gun mounting brackets; Auxiliary gaso-

RYAN

RYAN

(Above) PT-22A, originally ordered by the Dutch as seaplanes and ultimately delivered to the U. S. Army on wheels.

(Left) STM-2 in the markings of the Dutch Navy. Model-2 airframe on wheels.

(Below) Operational Ryan STM-S2 at Soerbaja Bay, Java in 1941.

T. POSTMA

Dutch Ryan STM-S2 operational in Java 1941. Most of these seaplanes were evacuated to Australia in 1942.

by the U. S. Army as PT-22s.

The Ryans were shipped in late 1940 through early 1941 on a number of Dutch ships. Operated in Java by "Wapen der Militaire Luchvaart van het Koninklijik Nederlands Indishe Legar" or ML for short, were 60 Army STM-E2 planes at Bandoeng (c/n 407-446, Dutch field numbers RO-10 through RO-49 and c/n 495-514, RO-50 through RO-60.) The 48 STM-S2 were used by the Dutch Naval Air Service, called "Marine Luchtvaart Dienst" or MLD. The Naval aircraft were operated on both wheels and floats, c/n 447-494, S-11 through S-58. The Dutch order left the factory with polished aluminum and silver wings. The national insignia was an orange inverted triangle bordered in black and the rudder painted in similar color.

Eight planes had been lost by December, 1941—two by fatal accidents on August 2 and 10—and S-42, c/n 479, by fire in October. Two more were destroyed by Japanese action February 3 and 17 and five more from unknown operational causes. All the Army Ryans at Bandoeng ultimately were lost and six were known to have been captured in flying condition. They were: c/n 407, RO-10; c/n 423, RO-26; c/n 425, RO-28; c/n 441, RO-44; c/n 445, RO-48; and c/n 510, RO-65.

A Dutch officer, Lt. H.F.C. Holts, who was taken captive on Java and managed to escape, tells this story in a Ryan company newsletter of 1943: "During this officer's imprisonment near Batavia Air Field, he saw the Japs using the Netherlands East Indies fleet of Ryan landplanes regularly for aerobatic training and formation flying. The one enjoyable sight

line tank; front cockpit cover; Blind flying hood and Beaching Gear.

No guns were known to have been mounted on any plane in this Dutch order at the factory or on the field.

One additional order, dated May 26, 1941, called for 25 Ryan ST-3 landplane trainers equipped with Menasco D4-B inline engines. This was, however, amended January 8, 1942, and called for 25 ST-3KR aircraft with Kinner R-55 (R-540-1) radial engines. They were c/n 1775 to 1779 and were never delivered to the Dutch but were ultimately purchased

he saw during his captivity was when two of the planes collided in midair as a result of poor piloting."

Twelve Dutch and an equal number of American instructors were training pilots at Maro Naval Base "little Pensacola." Seaplane operations were from Soerbaja Bay, which was just adjacent to the land base.

In another Ryan newsletter in1943, John H. Russell, an American instructor, tells some of his experiences with the Ryans in Java: "The Ryan trainers operated in the Netherlands East Indies were doing every possible job as military ships except gunnery and bombing training. They were primary, basic, advanced, and blind flying training all wrapped up in one; and our students went directly from Ryans to multi-engined equipment. And talk about acrobatic training! They're the sweetest acrobatic airplanes I've every flown.

"Our first class was a group of Dutch pilots who had had some instruction time in Holland before the invasion. They had escaped to England, and months later turned up in Java for further training.

"The landplane Ryans at Soerbaja Naval Base were flown inland about 50 miles to Malang when hostilities began. Our training course didn't include cross-country flying and many of the students who ferried the ships had as little as three hours time, so it was quite an expedition. It was no wonder that a number of the students ran out of gas because of poor navigation and made forced landings in sawahs (rice paddies), but the ships held up so well that in spite of several turn-overs none of the pilots were injured.

"Comparatively few airplanes were lost in training work, and all which were lost were with solo students, never instructors. In fact, American instructors took such a liking to the Ryan that three of us formed a stunt team to put on airshows for the Dutch to stimulate interest in their military pilot training program."

Earl "Chink" Lee, U. S. Navy flyer and an instructor in Ryans (his brother, Rollin Lee, worked for Ryan at San Diego), recalls a 25 minute dog fight between two Japanese fighters and one Ryan on floats, which returned to base full of holes and with his tab controls shot away. In a Ryan 1943 newsletter, he says: "Those Ryan seaplanes could really maneuver and easily turn inside of the Jap pursuits. Of course, they had no guns and had less than half the speed of the Japs, but they were so positive on control and so beautiful to handle in the air that this one pilot and others, too, are able to return from the one-sided dogfights, even though somewhat shot up.

"Actually some of the pilots felt so confident of the Ryans that in all seriousness they wanted to put 30 caliber machine guns on them and go out and engage the Jap fighters.

"One really effective use they found for the Ryans after things got too hot for training was to carry critically needed supplies to ships hidden in sheltered harbors, and supplies and medical supplies to outposts along the island coastline. Some of the STM-S2 seaplanes were also sent to Borneo early in the war to perform harbor patrol duty."

The ML had its Ryan at the Kali Djati Flight School 50 miles north of Bandoeng. When John Russell and the references in the Ryan Newsletter talk of Ryans at Bandoeng they mean the Kali Djati Flight School. On March 1, 1942, the Japanese overran the airfield defenses in a surprise attack a few hours after their landing on the Java coast. An unknown number of Ryans had been transferred to Tasikmalaja airfield during the end of Februrary, but all these planes were ultimately destroyed or captured.

On February 17 the remaining 34 Naval Aircraft were shipped aboard the M. S. Tjinegara in their original crates, their destination was Australia. Major parts from two other cannibalized seaplanes, S-16 and S-38, also were shipped.

In 1970, contact was made with the Imperial War Museum in Tokyo with the idea of gathering further information on the disposition of the captured Java and China Ryans. The answer, surprisingly enough, was quick to come from Japan. The letter gave overflight intelligence information gathered before the fall of Java on the number and type of planes used by the Dutch. Unfortunately, the Japanese considered the Ryans as trainers, and therefore "unworthy," so no inventory was even kept.

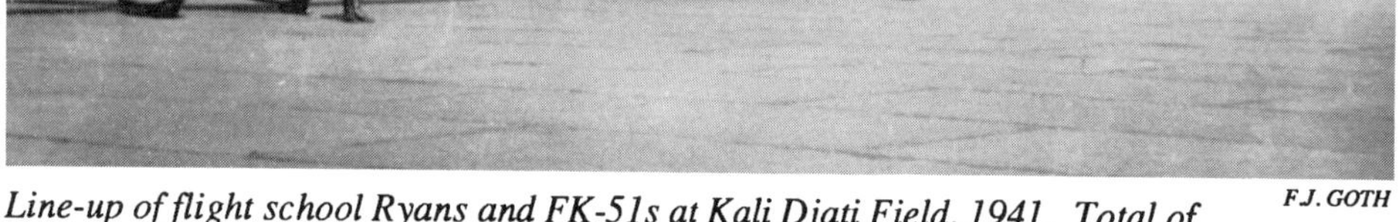

F.J. GOTH

Line-up of flight school Ryans and FK-51s at Kali Djati Field, 1941. Total of 60 were delivered to NEIAF as STM-2 and 48 to the Navy. 25 ST-3KRs powered with Kinner radials were repossessed in March 1942 by USAAF to become PT-22A (42-57479 through 57503).

Australian markings on STM-2, ex-Dutch Navy S-27. In service with 452 Sq. Richmond N.S.W., 1942. Also served with 5S.F.T.S., 1 Comm. Flt., General Recon. School and 2 A.O.S. RAAF

Australian Ryans

After arrival in Sydney, the Australian Ryans remained on the dock for a long period—March to July, 1942, before being moved to Mascot Aerodrome on July 21. The reported price paid for 34 planes and spares was $15,000.

One float plane version was operated at Rathmines, a Royal Australian Air Force Station. A few aircraft were assigned to numerous duty stations (BAGS, SFTC, 3CF, and WAG, etc.) which accounts for the fact that they were not painted in a uniform way. Most were used very little in the refresher training and transport missions of numbers 1, 2 and 3 Commissioned Fleets, General Reconnaissance Units.

To conserve avaition fuel, all the Ryans were decommissioned, their wings removed to ensure compliance, and stored at Evans Head. Then in April, 1945, a violent storm destroyed five of the airplanes.

With the war's end, the surviving 26 aircraft were sold by the Commonwealth Disposals Commission to Brown and Dureau, Ltd., on behalf of Corio Aviation Company. The average price was $400 each with engine or $200 without engine.

Four Ryans are known to have been fitted with de Havilland 140 hp "Gipsy Major" engines by Dave Bourke. This includes one civilian 1937 STA c/n 132, owned by Elmer L. Pickles. Dave owned STM, c/n 471, VH-BWQ, which he sold in 1975. He is considered the most knowledgeable man in Australia on Ryans. His designs for modifications of the center-section landing gear lugs for wire attachment and the stringer between bulkheads #2 and #3 are both required by DCA. Capt. Les Barnes was the owner of VH-AGR, c/n 475, which he flew out of Bankstown, near Sydney.

Laurie Smith badly damaged VH-AGD, c/n 459, in February, 1968, and sold the remains to Ian Baillie. On the left side of the #1 bulkhead, stamped into the skin, can be found identification number "11." Planes which have not been repaired in this area above the leveling angle, are marked with a number from 1 through 34. The Australians mistakenly think this is the Dutch number, which in reality is an RAAF marking referring to the plane's Australian field marking, A50-11.

Identification plates are riveted on the right side of the rear cockpit. They are the same as the

"New Ryan" plates used on civilian aircraft. I have owned three of these planes and have examined nine others. All are marked STM-S2. The airframes are built in accordance with all specifications of the civilian STA-Spl-2.

Ian Baillie's other Ryan, VH-AGV, is stored in America, having been sold to a Texan in 1970. Brushfires that burned many thousands of acres near Melbourne in 1968, and all of the houses and barns within ten miles of his home, were stopped inches from his private hangar and the Ryan was not harmed. The ship took three years to rebuild after having been "written off" on March 22, 1960, because of an accident.

There are a number of STM aircraft of which little or nothing is known. Two of these are Neil Hudson's VH-AHE and R. D. Soutar's VH-AHF, c/n 474 and 450 respectively. Both were Royal Newcastle Flying Club planes and were damaged many years ago. This flying club operated five Ryans in the late fifties. Ian Baillie bought most of the spare parts from the club when the Ryans were sold, but unfortunately the parts are of little use. They have been picked over for thirty years, and all of the often needed items are long gone. Many tail cones, tail feathers, crankcases, and flying wires remain, but no pistons, rings, wrist pins, spars, stub wings, or cowlings are left.

Bill Suhr modified c/n 465, VH-AGW, with a 150 Lycoming engine, a generator, Bayside radio and Cleveland brakes. The DCA would not allow an engine of greater power than the original. Although she flies well, the new owner is contemplating converting back to Menasco.

VH-AGZ, c/n 476, has had a diverse and traveled service life. After serving the Dutch as S-40 and flying for the RAAF as A50-30, it has made trips as a civilian from Australia to Tasmania and covered most of central and eastern Australia. It was owned by an outback grazer, Ewen MacKay, when I bought it. I flew it across the desert to the east coast and south to Sydney to be crated by Rex Aviation and shipped to the United States in 1969. This Ryan flew in Illinois as N288Y and then went to California in a United Air Lines DC-8 freighter. The current owner is Mitch Mayborn in Texas; the registration has been changed to N7779.

Three Ryans worked in Hong Kong for flight training. They were all registered but not flown in Australia previously. The first of these is c/n 452, VH-AGY, in Australia and then VR-HDL in Hong Kong. Then it went to Norway and flew as LN-TVF. This plane was bought in 1967 by Capt. James Bassett, USAF, and shipped to New York where it remained stored until 1969. That winter it was flown west as N9761 to Oregon.

The story of the second plane, VH-AGX, and then VR-HDM, was routine up to the time it was ditched in Kowloon Bay. It was salvaged and fitted with a radial engine similar to the PT-22 and used for ground instructional purposes only. Derelict for years, it was bought in the early 1970s and shipped to an American in Tacoma, Washington. The third Hong Kong Ryan, c/n 494, left China for the Phillippines and has been registered as PI-C324 and PI-471. The engine was changed to a modern Lycoming O-435. Number 494 is now flying in America, again behind a Menasco and with an old STA registration N14911.

Another Java-Aussi Ryan that went to the U. S. is c/n 451. It made a forced landing on a Brisbane beach and was rebuilt by B. G. Andersen. In thirty years it had only flown 324 hours. Shipped by air to Sydney in a Bristol Freighter and then by sea to New York, it now flies in Illinois and is owned by Mrs. Robert Friedman who still has it painted in original Dutch colors as S-21.

Ryan c/n 454 suffered a fatal crash at Bankstown, New South Wales, April 6, 1961. This was a freak accident in which the passenger was killed by a splinter of plexiglass from the broken windshield when the Ryan failed to clear some trees on a landing approach. A few parts are still stored from it, but not enough to ever see it fly again.

John Banger's VH-RAE was one of two Gipsy powered Ryans still flying. This aircraft, c/n 467, is the only one ever licensed without the landing wire reinforcement and has in its place a flying wire, braced between the landing gear "V" struts. Unfortunately, it was wrecked in a very strange manner. The owner was checking out a friend in the ST. Both thought the other had the controls. Oblivious to the fact that the aircraft was "flying itself," neither pilot had noticed that they were gradually converging with a set of three power lines which ran between two farms. At the last moment, both pilots saw the power lines, but it was too late. The aircraft hit the wires, skidded along them for a short distance, and was flung sideways to the ground. It struck with its port wing tip, cartwheeled, and came to rest upside down in a corn field. Both pilots escaped with minor injuries. VH-RAE has a new owner who plans on putting it back in the air by combining the usable parts with a hulk from Central Technical College in Brisbane.

Val Chapman has two well cared for Ryans in Jeriderie, New South Wales. VH-AHC is fitted with front seat long range fuel tanks, while VH-AHD is of standard configuration. Val has owned them for over twenty years, always keeping the aluminum polished. Also at Jeriderie is Dr. A. Fisher's red VH-CXR, c/n 482, which is now the only flying STM with a Gipsy engine.

Chapter Eight

"Put" Humphreys flying Tex Rankin's STA. Note the long pipe on belly for smoke trails.

Flying the Ryan ST

On the ground the ST is not easy to handle either on takeoff or landing. Taxiing requires skill and a feel, as it will not respond to the usual rudder control. A combination of rudder and light repeated jabs on the brakes will turn it handily and even hold it in a cross wind. Forward visibility is nil and continual S turns are in order.

Takeoff is usually no problem when the power is fed slowly. Some rudder is needed to overcome torque at all speeds and altitudes except normal cruise speed. The ST will leave the ground at about 50 mph at full throttle in a rather long takeoff roll. They are not known for their short takeoffs. The usual rate of climb is 80 mph, with a normal cruise speed of 120 mph for the STA and 130 mph for the STA-Spl. There is approximately 90 mph difference between takeoff speed and cruise speed. It is easily handled and responsive in the air and has absolutely no bad habits. These are some of the main factors that make the Ryan STA a true sports plane.

It is possible to spin the Ryan, but this can only be done intentionally. In a spin it will recover almost immediately, and stalls can be caught before the nose falls through the horizon.

One inherent feature of the ST, which the military in particular did not like, was the need to cross control the ailerons in some banked turns. Having to hold the left rudder and right aileron in a left turn is confusing to a low time student. The later ST-3 aircraft did not have this characteristic.

Experienced pilots do not even notice the need to cross control under these circumstances and do it automatically. It does not tend to lose much aileron response in slow flight, and cross-controlling will not make it spin. With the flaps down one, two, or three notches, aileron response is still good at low speeds.

Four notches should not be used for landing because this causes an air flow interference with the ailerons and the rate of sink is too great without use of a lot of power.

The Ryan is a good aerobatic plane for pleasure, but not for competition above Novice or Sportsman categories. It will perform rolling maneuvers smoother than anything in the air, albeit at a rate that leaves something to be desired. You can start a loop at a low speed of only 110 mph and still not lose any altitude completing it. Hammerheads, slow rolls, Cuban eights, and snap rolls are a delight. Climbing maneuvers such as vertical rolls are a disaster; the ST just cannot do them.

Landing requires the pilot to stay alert. The big problem is overcontrolling the rudder. It is best to use very little rudder, and make some horizontal correction with the ailerons. A left slip with three notches of flaps and 25% power at 60 mph is the way most like to make approaches. The slip is so you have forward visibility. The power with this much flap will make it stop flying in a three point landing when it is chopped.

The wing wires are excellent air speed indicators. When adjusted correctly the rear top wire will start to vibrate at about 65 mph and the front wire at 50 mph. These wires are in plain view of the pilot and to look at the air speed requires you to glance away briefly. This is a proven technique because when the nose comes up for a landing, forward visibility is cut off and most pilots need all the help they can get at this time.

Just before touching down you must straighten out. Once on the ground, the roll out is the hardest part of controlling these early Ryans, particularly on a hard surface runway. Use the rudder sparingly as the steerable tail wheel will disconnect easily, leaving you with only brakes to keep her straight. The rudder at low roll out speeds has little effect anyway, and moving it hard to one side or the other will make it impossible to get your heel on the brakes. The trick is to leave your heel on the brake pedals at all times when landing, and use the rudder as little as possible, giving the brakes short jabs when needed. As you will find later when reading the opinions of the other pilots, their methods will differ considerably.

The Department of Commerce issued a manual for the Civilian Pilot Training program in November, 1940, for the Ryan STA. "As a result of extensive operating experience it has been found satisfactory to increase slightly the recommended maximum speeds of entry for some of the maneuvers."

Maneuver	*Recommended Max. Speed of Entry*
Snap Roll	90 mph
Vertical Reversement	80 mph
Loop	140 mph
Immelman	140 mph
Slow Roll	125 mph
Never Exceed Speed	170 mph

Note: The aircraft is placarded for a never exceed speed of 156 mph.

Generally, the performance is less than advertised. The maximum cruising range with any reasonable reverse is about 240 miles at 120 mph with a rate of climb at gross (70°) of only 600 ft/min., which is half the advertised rate. The service ceiling is no more than 14,000 ft. The average ST-1-2 weighs approximately 1,105 lbs. empty without radio, starter or generator.

The STC information for the STA-Spl (page 154, Aircraft Listings) shows data for both open and closed cabin land planes (PO-CLM). Why then were there only two factory orders for the cockpit enclosure? With cabin planes the coming thing, this may have seemed strange, but then really it was not.

The problem was in the tandem seating arrangement and the angle at which the pilot must look through the plexiglass. When the nose came up, the pilot changed his forward view for one in which he looked through the side panels. Plexiglass has so much distortion when looking through it at an angle that it required opening the sliding hatch. This is not reasonable in a civilian's aircraft, particularly in the winter. The hatch covers are expensive, hence only one was sold. At least three STAs had homemade enclosures at one time or another.

Bill Dodd and his ex-Guatemalian STM, N11, was used in acrobatic exhibitions at fly-ins and air shows more than any other Ryan. His flying was almost flawless. The little orange and silver Ryan would loop and roll through sequences laid out to show the best in an already good aircraft. He won the Amateur Aerobatic Championship at Ottumwa three years running, 1961-62-63.

His Ryan was equipped with an inverted fuel system and a cut-out in the rear cockpit to make room for a back-pack parachute. His flying was so good that it looked deceivingly easy. The registration of this Ryan was changed in 1972, to N302D.

The following are some excerpts from an article by Bill Dodd that was first printed in the *ANTIQUER*, January 1966.

"On takeoff the pilot should content himself with doing almost nothing with the rudder except progressively pushing a little on the right one as take off run begins. In a good stiff cross wind, the best method is to control the first part of takeoff by holding the tail down by back stick until good speed is attained and the rudder will do the controlling.

"It doesn't come in like a streamlined brick and doesn't land especially hot. Without flaps, it approaches best at about 75 mph indicated. The attitude is almost straight and level with the rate of descent not at all excessive. Touchdown is at about 50 mph. If you want to come down more steeply and at a lower speed, you can choose 10, 20, 30 or 45 degress of flaps by pulling on the conveniently located manual flap handle on the right. Just depress the button at the top of the handle and let go when you get the slot you want. To release, simply do the procedure in reverse. Make a habit when you pull the flap on to wiggle the handle to be sure it has locked solidly in the chosen slot. Once long ago I didn't do that and at 20 ft. on the flareout the flaps popped back to zero. There was no emergency. The ST simply sank a little and floated faster and farther down the runway. So once again we have an example of the Ryan not doing something violent.

"The main distinguishing feature of the ST is the roll out on landing. Everything is smooth and normal after touchdown until it starts to slow down at which point the nose wants to wander to one side or the other, which requires quick alternate rudder action. Everything is OK again for a while until you begin to realize you could use a small assist from the brakes—just in case.

"The cockpit is clean, neat, somewhat Spartan in its simplicity but quite utilitarian. There is everything there that is needed but nothing more. The controls are simple. The elevator trim tab, for example, is a small cable that runs through the cockpit just under the throttle. Three pulls forward or back gives full up or down trim. This is a very good feature for aerobatics when quick trimming is needed during or between maneuvers.

"In the air, for just flying around, you will look a long time to find a plane which flies so smoothly, stably and with such good visibility.

"Stalling from any attitude, even inverted, is a delight. It simply stalls and drops off lazily and recovers quickly with any help at all. If, however, it is held in tight, it will reluctantly spin. The spin is really something! It points straight down as if on a spit and really winds up.

"The stall and quick spin recovery once again prove to you that this is definitely not a violent airplane. If you were to apply one word to the Ryan ST, it would have to be 'predictable.'

"As for aerobatic maneuvers, the ST will do them all, inside and outside, both basic and advanced. The airfoil, which is an NACA 2412, has a good curve to the bottom for excellent outside loop and inverted flight characteristics. It has, indeed a very good rate of roll, which surprises most people who think that single stock ailerons can't be that good.

"The only two maneuvers I've found the Ryan doesn't do as well as I'd like is an outside snap and a vertical roll.

"Most models of STs that I've flown indicate between 110 and 120 mph depending on horsepower and props. The specs list the dive limit speed at 156 mph. However, many instructors who operated Menasco-powered Ryan trainers for the Air Force, with whom I've talked, say they have had 215-220 indicated on air speeds many times when students went completely to sleep during aerobatics. And too, we personally have had outs up to 210 to test the truth of this. The wings flap a bit, the wires sing like banshees, the wind whistles, but there was no big vibration or buffeting and it coasted out to a more comfortable speed."

The well known John "Tex" Rankin also had something to say about his STA in the September 1937 issue of *AVIATION* magazine. Unfortunately, either he was misquoted or was overstressing both his aircraft and the Menasco engine. The entry speeds for maneuvers and engine speeds quoted by him should be considered dangerous and foolish. I have paranthetically added the maxiumum speeds recommended by the factories.

"The plane I used at St. Louis, and which I am using in all my aerobatic exhibitions, moving picture flying, and student work is a stock Ryan STA monoplane powered with a stock Menasco C-4 125 hp engine. Monoplanes have not ordinarily been used for aerobatics but I have found the ship ideal for such work and it is my impression that the last stronghold of the biplane type has now been successfully invaded. The only special equipment on the plane is a

front cockpit cover, a Kollsman sensitive altimeter, and a small telephone number finder on the dashboard to carry a tape upon which I diagram my complete program, which I unroll by hand as the maneuvers are completed. My Menasco engine has no special provision for continuous operation in inverted flight. In fact the oil pressure drops to zero every time the ship is put into an inverted position. The engine manufacturer would probably not commend this practice but after 300 hours of aerobatic work, with power drives to 300 mph (red line 156) and engine rpm to 3500 (red line 2160) and with the plane often upside down, no major overhaul has yet been necessary. For carburation when I inverted, I selected a hand fuel pump from an old wrecked Cadillac and installed this in the cockpit properly connected to draw fuel from the tank and meter it into the carburetor intake through a special jet. Before going into inverted flight I will fill this pump (if I forget the engine quits running very shortly) then, when on my back, I maintain carburation by a steady pressure on the pump handle.

"By long experience with the Ryan I have learned the ideal speed for every maneuver. For example, an outside loop out of inverted position has a normal diameter of 1200 ft. and a maximum speed of 280 mph (140 mph) at the bottom of the loop. The Ryan can be outside looped within a 700 ft. diameter and at speeds as low as 175 mph, but the maneuver is smoother and there is less strain on the ship when holding to the 1200 ft. diameter and a maximum speed of 240-280 mph. A single snap roll works best at 90 mph and a double snap roll at 118 mph. A vertical snap roll with the Ryan is best if done at a speed of 140 mph. These speeds, once established, should never be varied. The pilot must learn the feel *of his controls in order to determine the ideal speed for each maneuver, and he must also learn to watch his airspeed indicator in order to hold that speed consistently. I handle the controls very easily on any plane, never under any circumstance applying them hard at speeds above 150 mph."*

Ernest K. Gann, the well known aviation writer, had early experience with an STA (NC16042, c/n 131) that was owned by his employer, Joe Lewis, of Lewis Air Service and referred to in this narrative as Logan. The date was 1937 and this quote is from Gann's book *FLYING CIRCUS*, first printed in 1975. We reprint Gann's impressions with the kind permission of Macmillan Publishing Co., Inc.

"The Ryan is a wonderful partner, and while it is different to picture Logan as an extraordinarily sensitive man, his aerial ballets are more than thrilling. They are pure art.

"The Ryan is a low-wing monoplane powered by a Menasco engine. The fuselage is of metal, the wings and empennage of fabric; it is capable of any acrobatic I know and forgiving enough to rescue me from certain cavortings I do not know, yet persist in trying. Loops in a Ryan are routine, of course. I can go around repeatedly making the circles round instead of egg shaped and easily keep the identical top and bottom altitudes for each revolution. The Ryan also spins smartly and without viciousness. Absolute accuracy in recovery is easy. Snap rolls can be repeated without loss of altitude again and again until you work off a mood or find it necessary to stuff your eyes back in your head. Symmetrically smooth rolls are more difficult. I cannot seem to manage one unless I start with a dive, which robs the action of grace...

"I pull down my goggles because the instant the Ryan is on its back, various bits of debris will certainly find my face. It doesn't seem to make any difference how many times I sweep the cockpit flooring; once the Ryan is on its back, from somewhere, pebbles, dust, gum wrappers, or even one of Logan's cigar butts will find its way through the various openings and float past my face...

"The engine begins its sputtering which it always does when inverted...

"When the Menasco's fuel system is again stabilizied, I roll the Ryan over on her back, pull the stick momentarily, and "Split S" into a vertical dive to six thousand feet. The beautiful wilderness aloft is now forgotten. The Ryan and I are open for the morning's business. On the way down, while the Menasco resumes sputtering, I consider dutifully the folly of acrobatics without parachute..."

The PT-22 was a superb military trainer mainly because it flies like a brick and has most of the nasty habits of a much heavier plane. No cross controlling was necessary. It taxied easily and did nothing without full warning to even a low time student that was properly instructed. You are not doing a Dodo (Army student pilot) any favors teaching him to fly in a light, delicate, forgiving sport plane like a Ryan STA. He will be flying P-40's and other heavy aircraft and the "22" was near perfect training.

There are no noticeably bad torque problems on the takeoff and lift is usually about 65 mph. Never pull the nose up until at least 80 mph is attained and make no pattern turns at more than 15 degrees and at less than 95 mph.

Flying idiosyncrasies were built into this plane by added weight and the sweep back to the wings. A long flight with a good instructor, at high altitude and with parachutes, is a must to fully understand and get the treu feel of this strange, wonderful bird.

Try and set up a straight and level cruise speed and then with a 15 degree bank make a turn. Hold your altitude and continue the turn, watching and feeling for slight buffeting as your airpseed drops. If, at this point, you add power or drop your nose, nothing will happen, but if you don't the plane will stall and spin. Normally this "gentle" type of spin of less than one turn can be caught and you can be in level flight again in about 600 feet.

A few words of caution concerning the spin: the ST stops spinning easily and will start again in the other direction unless the rudder is neutralized at precisely the right moment. The aircraft angle when spinning is almost straight down and it will really wind up. The center of the first turn is about 300 ft. off the nose, the second turn 10 ft., and the third turn you are turning on your spinner.

High speed stalls are fantastic in the ST-3 and can be done at any speed or attitude. The best way to demonstrate this type of stall is in a 720° turn at full rpm. Slowly pull back the stick when in about a 45° bank. She starts by buffeting hard, offering you warning and then the horizon will go by so fast as it lets go that a new "22" pilot will hardly believe it!

It is possible to high speed stall this plane and not spin it. Put it into a shallow dive as if starting a loop and then about 145 mph pull back rather suddenly on the stick. The aircraft will not even get the nose straight up before it stalls. The "G" meter can read up to about four in the maneuver, but you need not worry about the plane. It is stressed at 10 positive and 8 negative.

There is one flight attitude in which the PT-22 is really bad. This is slow flight. It is totally intolerant of the pilot who makes turns, cross controls and roughly handles the ailerons during slow flight. The best training for this condition is to control the roll only with rudder as long as possible without falling off on one wing.

As you see, most of the problems occur when the aircraft is in an attitude as if landing. The flaps add one more difficulty. They will accelerate the problems and if they slip from full down to full up, suddenly the plane will sink about 100 ft. before recoving. If the pilot were to give full throttle at this time and any correction with the aileron, it would most likely snap roll.

Aerobatic training is carried out in these planes and is comparatively safe at high altitude because the ships are built very well and stressed for high G loads. It would be extremely foolish for even an expert to try to get a low level waiver for the PT-22. Although it can basically complete most maneuvers, a considerable loss of altitude will result. A pilot competing in even Novice category will be at a disadvantage against even such marginal aerobatic planes as a Citabria. A fun plane it is! A sports plane, top aerobatic plane, it is not. Take the ST-3 for what it is, an old surplus Primary Trainer; fly "by the book" and keep it healthy and shining. Your reward will be the time of your life. The PT-22 will do many things suddenly, but never without considerable warning to a reasonably good pilot.

Approaches for landing are made at 90 mph. There are no particular difficulties in roll-out because of the wide track gear and the toe brakes. Paved airports are no problem.

One pertubing item is the sound of the Kinner engine; it always seems rough and missing. If you hold your head to one side of the cockpit and then the other in flight the sound will change from a smooth roar to sharp individual explosions. The five cylinder radial is equipped with an exhaust collector for the carburetor heat on two cylinders and short open stacks for the others.

Many accidents plagued the PT-22 after World War II. Most could be directly attributed to poor maintenance and a total lack of understanding of the flight characteristics of this surplus trainer. The bad reputation not only followed the PT-22 but spilled over on the STA's. Most people really do not know the difference, as they have usually never even seen an early Ryan.

A large number of photographs showing PT-21 accidents, their causes and fatalities were obtained from Bill Richards. These pictures are a photographic record kept by the civilian maintenance personnel at King City, California, Palo Alto Field in 1942. They tell a great deal about the PT-21, the most interesting being that stall spin accidents were only about 5% of the total. This means that the Army could teach low time students how to avoid this plane's only really dangerous characteristic. This fact leaves one reasonable conclusion possible. If the Army could fly the PT-22 safely, then there is little reason why civilians cannot do the same.

In May, 1943, Aviation Cadet D. J. Armand reported for flight training in PT-22's. He was a member of Cadet Class 43-K, Fifth Army Air Forces Training Detachment at Ryan Field, Hemet, California. The following is reprinted in part from the National Ryan Club Newsletter, April, 1973, and a letter dated February, 1976, from Dr. Armand:

"The sight of those PT-22s in the traffic pattern was a thrill, and I'm sure many of my classmates had a few feelings of apprehension as I did about our ability to handle this little monster.

"During our pre-flight training at Santa Ana, we had heard barracks talk by the carload on the relative merits of the three preliminary trainers then in use, the PT-19, PT-17, and the PT-22. Though the Stearman was touchy during the landing roll, neither it nor the Fairchild landed as fast as the Ryan, so the stories went. By the time we were told where we would go for primary training, we were pumped so full of talk that those of us who were assigned to Ryans firmly believed we would be landing a P-40 on our first flight. So, it was both a matter of concern and at the same time, a challenge.

"My first flight, or orientation flight, came on May 26, 1943, and it was also the first time I had ever been up in any aircraft. The entry in my log book shows 'Army PT-22, H.P. 160, No. 484-A' (Field Number). The flight lasted 35 minutes and consisted mostly of my being shown the local flying area and our auxiliary fields. I was allowed to take the controls for a considerable part of the time and began my actual flying training by doing a series of turns. Though I had never actually flown before, I was no stranger to aircraft and the functions of their controls.

"The flight instructors at Hemet were all civilian, but dressed in uniforms and were treated by all cadets as commissioned officers. My instructor, Mr. J. F. Hutchins, was a fine gentleman, soft-spoken and easy going. He never got ruffled; even in hairy situations you could always depend on that calm, quiet voice over the gosport to help you out. To me at that time, an impressionable 19-year-old who lived, breathed and dreamed of airplanes, he was only second to God.

"My second flight came on May 29, in number 595, and lasted 40 minutes. This time I was allowed to follow through on the controls during takeoff and after then it was mine. We climbed to our working area and I began practicing turns again. Later on Mr. Hutchins demonstrated power-on and power-off stalls, straight ahead, and let me try some. The last item on that flight before landing was my first introduction to what I thought at the time was a complete disaster—the spin.

"There was a requirement at Hemet on the Ryans that no one would be allowed to solo with less than eight hours dual, no matter how much previous time he had. Since I passed this minimum and had had my cross-check, I knew my solo was not too far away, so I was getting pretty excited.

"The next day, June 19, we took off in number 832 and went to one of our auxiliary fields. As I remember, there were three or four of these fields, which were sod, where we did our practice takeoffs and landings in order to relieve the load at the main field. There was a small stage-house in a corner, where a caretaker usually sat during the day, and where an instructor could sit while his student shot solo landings. After I shot a couple of landings, Mr. Hutchins told me to taxi over to the stage-house. When I stopped, he climbed out of the front pit, stepped down off the wing and said, "You're ready; want it?" I gulped and nodded, so he walked away.

"Back to the takeoff position I went, with a feeling that something was not the same. It was not until I was about 300 ft. in the air that I realized what it was. That familiar head was missing from the front pit.

"On June 22, I had my ten-hour check ride during which I did steep turns, stalls and S's along a road. Immediately following that, I had a 30-minute period of dual on 90° spot landings, after which I went solo for 45-minutes more to practice.

"My 30-hour check ride came on July 2 and my log book showed a total of 31 hours, 30 minutes. The ride lasted 30 minutes; then I had two more solo hops that day. The next day brought one hour of dual with some aerobatics; snap rolls and slow rolls.

"All the Ryans at Hemet, except one, were painted with yellow wings and tails and the fuselages were left the natural aluminum color. That one ship, number 780, was the personal ship of Lieutenant Raymond V. Castro, one of the Army check pilots. It was all silver, and always shone like a new coin. On July 8, with 45 hours and 15 minutes of time so far, I took my Army check ride with Lieutenant Castro. It lasted 25 minutes and consisted of a spin, some stalls, chandelles, snap rolls and a couple of landings.

"The aircraft I flew at Hemet Field, California in 1943 were, of course, still relatively new and well maintained, so there were very few mechanical failures. I don't remember anyone in my class having very few mechanical failures. I don't remember anyone in my class having a forced landing because of engine failure. Though the Kinner was a dependable engine, it just wasn't enough power for the Ryan. To

me, this was the weak point of the ship. It was okay for routine flying, but it didn't have enough oomph for aerobatics. I've often wondered how the plane would have performed with the 220 hp Continental which the stearman PT-17 had.

"The landing gear was a strong point on the Ryan. It was wide enough to help prevent loops if you stayed on your toes, even in cross wind landings where you were required to three-point it. And it was an extremely rugged gear, absorbing the pounding of countless hard landings without any appreciable damage.

"Staying in the traffic pattern and shooting landings was what I liked best. As long as you flew the Ryan and didn't let it fly you, you had no sweat. Keep the nose down and airspeed constant when reducing power on the final turn. The ship had a solid feel on the final, and as you pumped down the flaps you could feel it "roll" over them while you pushed the nose down a little more. If the air was calm, it was a joy to land. When you cut the power to flare out, assuming your speed was right, it didn't fool around with a long, drawn out float but settled quite firmly to the ground. That hollow drumming sound from the metal fuselage was sweet music to your ears, but it didn't mean you could stop flying it. That didn't stop until you had parked and cut the switch.

"In air work, I found the Ryan to be a pretty good performer, with the power at hand. It was just heavy enough to have a solid feel in the air, with good control response. If you flew a good coordinated airplane and watched your speed, you could go through all the maneuvers required in our training without any real trouble. The only place I remember a rather violent reaction out of the Ryan was in steep turns, when you fed in too much top or bottom rudder. It would snap into a spin awfully fast. After going through that a few times, we were real careful in making our final turn in the traffic pattern.

"To sum up, I think the Ryan was a great little ship. It was rugged, dependable and well suited to accomplish the mission of training military pilots who would move along to more sophisticated, powerful and heavy aircraft. It had its own built-in traits which instilled at an early stage awareness to be on your toes at all times. Respect the little beast, but always be master of it.

"As we neared the time when our primary training would be finished, our instructors demanded better and better performance. All maneuvers had to be executed smoothly and precisely, within the limits allowed that poor 160 hp Kinner. I had reached an understanding by now with the Ryan, and looked forward to each new flight with a great deal of anticipation. We had been checked out on all the required maneuvers and our flights were now practice and more practice. I remember the 90° crosswind landing especially, because we were required to three-point it in all except a severe wind. Surprisingly, we had very few ground loops. In fact, while 43-K was at Hemet, there was only one accident I recall. It involved one of the 43-J students on a solo flight, and he died in the crash."

Tex Rankin and T. Claude Ryan with NC14914. RYAN

Ryan PT-20.

RYAN AERONAUTICAL LIBRARY

PARAMOUNT

HE FLIES THROUGH THE AIR - Joseph Allen, Paramount player starred with Jean Cagney (James' sister) in "Campus Wives," knew what to do when the weather was hot and he had a few hours of free time. He got in a plane and went flying.

Cockpit of the ST-A, control stick and wing flap levers were chrome plated.

Chapter Nine

N. A. "Monk" Nabell, short time factory manager, and STA, NC14952, c/n 108. RYAN

Construction Details for ST-1 and ST-2

Many construction details of the ST aircraft were ahead of their time. The first sketches were of a rather contemporary plane with a straight turtle-back, wide cord short wings and powered by an in-line Cirrus engine. The details were refined by two Ryan engineers, Willard Boyd and Will Vandermeir, under the direction of T. Claude Ryan.

Years later Claude Ryan was asked about the influence that two well known low-wing designs of the time had on his own design. According to William Wagner, the Gee Bee racer was ". . . these and other racers of that period were the inspiration to me for the configuration of the ST." The construction of the landing gear, wings, and tail bear considerable similarities.

"If the P-26 had any direct influence I am not aware of it," Mr. Ryan continued, "but naturally, any designer is bound to keep up on the latest aircraft and can be influenced without even being aware. The Gee Bee, however, seems to have more direct influence."

At least five engines were considered for the prototype ST. The Wright 90 hp Gypsy, Menasco B4 95 hp, and the Menasco C4 125 hp were the front runners. The actual reason for the choice is not known, but Claude Ryan was a friend of Al Menasco and later remarked, "As an airplane manufacturer I have long recognized the sound engineering, the stamina and the high performance of Menasco engines which we are now using and have been using for several years."

The cowling for the Menasco lends itself to beautiful streamlining and a very small frontal area. The engine advertisements pushed this fact and one of Menasco's slogans was, "You wouldn't shoot a bullet sideways." Their other slogan, often seen, was "You

RYAN

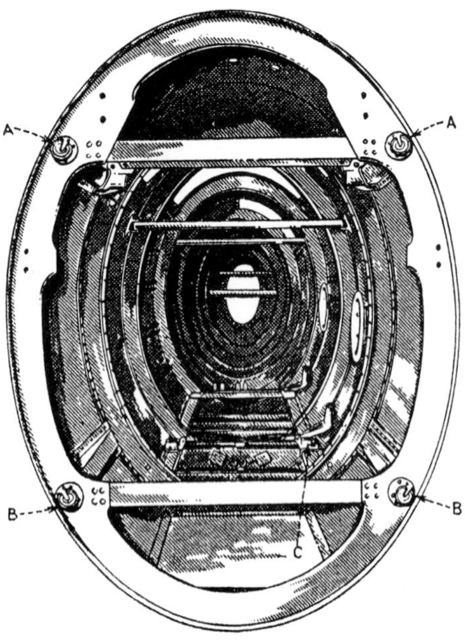

RYAN

(Above Left) c/n 101 on wooden jig with stub-wing ribs in place.

(Above Right) The fuselage of the Ryan ST is of semi-monocoque construction with four main longerons.

(Left) Completed right wing, less aluminum leading edge.

can't fly cross country at sea level," in reference to the supercharged version of the engine.

The first prototype was built with the help of Ryan A&P students and a small shop crew, the nucleus of which was Mel Thompson, Bert Mathews, Ed Morrow, Bob Kerlinger, W. M. "Mac" Cattrell, and James Fornasero. These were all under the direction of Dan Burnette, a very competent engineer in his own right, and one who would prove his worth many times over as a Ryan employee.

The Fuselage (less the engine compartment) was built in two parts. Both were eventually semi-monocoque. The forward cockpit area had four stringers running the full length. Two were inside under the cockpit opening and two supported the floor boards. The construction of this area of the fuselage remained the same throughout ST-1 and ST-2 production with one modification, that of changing the cockpit stringers to the outside to make more interior room in the model-2 aircraft.

The tail cone area was monocoque construction, at first only using three "stringers" formed by a 90° bend inward of one inch on each underlying skin. The later aircraft, after 1937, had a "hat" section in the form of two real stringers between bulkheads #4 and #7. All aircraft that are flying have had these stringers either built into them at the factory or were modified by Service Bulletin #6.

The skin is 24ST .032 thick and fabricated from flat sheets. The beautiful streamlining, cowl work and fillets give the impression of compound curved sections to the whole fuselage but this is an illusion. All bulkheads are stamped aluminum with the exception of #2 and the bottom half of #3, which were heat treated 4130 steel.

If one phrase were to characterize this aircraft construction it would have to be "hand made." Every part was cut, fitted, welded, formed, etc., by hand. With the exception of the engine and wheels, almost nothing is machine made. For the middle 1930s, this

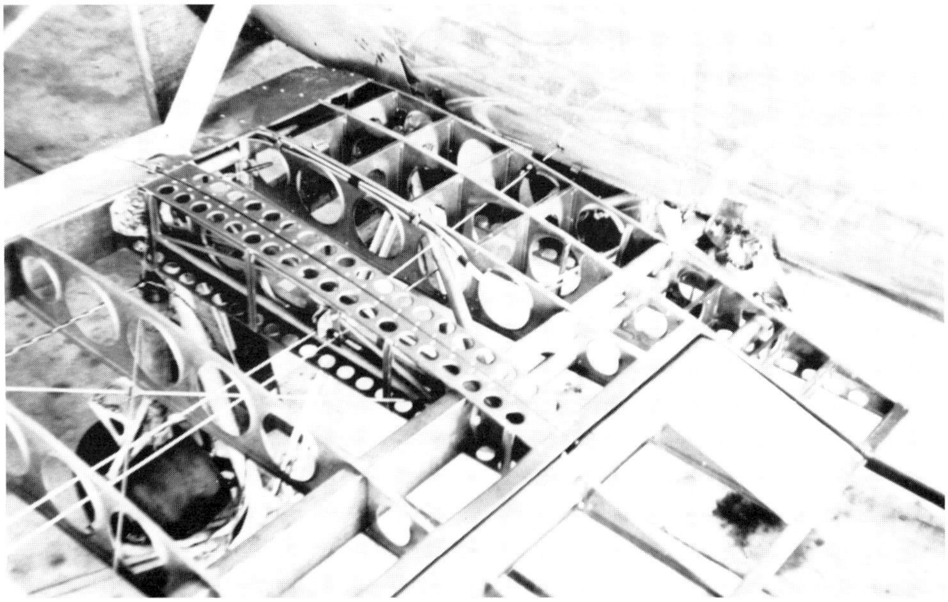
RYAN

Wing and wing stub detail, early aircraft with long crank operated flaps that extend into stub-wing.

was an excellent way to produce a few aircraft cheaply, but it spelled the end to this series of Ryans when skilled labor became scarce at the start of World War II.

The Wings were made with solid spruce spars and mated with 13 stamped aluminum alloy ribs. Eight steel compression ribs with five bays of drag and anti-drag wires and a thin (.016) aluminum leading edge made up a very strong wing. This leading edge was too thin and looked bad under the fabric in a very short time. It is a good idea when fabric needs replacing to reskin the leading edge with .020, 2024, 3T alclad. The airfoil section is NACA 2412 and remained constant throughout production of all ST-1,ST-2 and ST-3 models.

One misconception that continually appears in print about the ST-1, ST-2 and ST-3 concerns the use of ball bearings for the control surfaces. There are *no* ball bearings in any control surface and omitting the wheels and engine there are only two ball bearings in the airframe. These are located under and just forward of the rear pilot seat in the pulleys that guide the elevator cables.

Flaps and Ailerons are constructed with a steel tube spar which also serves as a bearing surface. The female portions are bronze blocks. These were very coarse bearings, but served their purpose well and were exceptionally light and smooth to the touch in flight. The ribs were stamped aluminum with a trailing edge also of aluminum.

The early ST-1 aircraft, through c/n 119 (19th plane built), had long flaps that extended into the stubwing area and were controlled by a small crank in the rear cockpit only. A lever replaced the crank and was a great improvement with its instant response, and the shorter flaps did not change the flying characteristics in any way. In fact, there is no mention of it in the STC; this was the only major change throughout the production of this model.

Tail surfaces in all six parts were constructed basically the same. The spars were steel tubes, the ribs were stamped aluminum, and the trailing edges are small aluminum tubes. The hinges are made from three small sections of thick wall tubing (one welded to a rudder, for instance), and two welded to a vertical stabilizer with a bolt through them. Again, these serve well but have only poor provisions to take up for wear and bolts have to be replaced periodically.

None of these surfaces are counterbalanced.

RYAN

Tail cone and stabilizer parts. Note wooden patterns on wall from which stamping dies are manufactured.

NC14952, c/n 108, being crated for shipment to Hawaii. RYAN

The rudder "clamshells," or fairings, are not integral to the rudder and can be removed for service of the tailwheel area. They have no effect on the flying qualities. Trimming tabs located on both elevators are aluminum and are controlled by a continuous wire running through both cockpits and a worm screw mechanism located in the tail cone. They are simple, trouble free, and easy to operate.

Tail wheels were known to have been made in at least three variations. The first was full swivel with no locking unit and a trombone type shock absorber utilizing two small bungees. The second, again with the trombone shock, featured a steerable tail wheel with an unlocking unit that unlocked the rudder when the wheel differed in direction more than 45°. Last, and most common, was a plunger and spring shock unit coupled with an unlocking steerable tail wheel. The tire and wheel were both Goodyear, eight inch streamlined.

Stub wings are steel tube assemblies welded and sealed after being oil treated on the inside. The only heat treated units in the stub wings were the rear spar which is built up and Z braced with double tubes. The early ST-1 had a wing walk on the left side only and the walk itself was plywood over heavier aluminum ribs. The first 19 airplanes had the cutout for the long wing flaps and had one hinge support for the flap. Some of the STM-1 aircraft had a wing walk on both stub wings and the walk was sheet aluminum covered. The last variant was a special corrugated walk support on both sides as found only on ST-2 and ST-3. The front spar of each stub wing has been reported as being larger on the seaplane trainer model STM-S2. On the one aircraft we were able to examine, this was not the case.

Landing gear is the treadle type employing Goodyear air wheels 18" x 8" x 3". The brakes are a multiple disc mechanical type operated by heel brake pedals in both cockpits. The late aircraft, ST-2, had toe brakes and parking brakes. The main shock units were Cleveland Air Oil. The first prototype had wheel pants split from front to rear and all production aircraft also had a front and rear section.

Engine compartment with a steel tube mount accepted six models of Menascos (B4, C4, D4, D4-87, C4S and C4S-2). The early oil tanks were 2 gallon with louvers in the top cowl for cooling. They were replaced by 2 1/2 gallon and then 2 3/4 gallon tanks. The Menascos had a tendency toward high oil temperature and the larger tanks and the oil radiator on the C4S models generally corrected this problem. Only the prototype had a ground adjustable aluminum propeller. It was used for only one flight and was then replaced with a wood blade propeller on all production models.

RYAN
Only the first ST, c/n 101, had wheel pants split from front to rear.

Accomodations were tandem open cockpits with one piece curved plexiglass windshields, which were small and sloping on early aircraft with small cockpit openings. Later planes, c/n 307 and up, and those modified by Alteration Bulletin #7, have larger cockpit openings and much larger windshields. Construction Number 340 and subsequent aircraft are considered ST-2s. They are equipped with dual flap handles, parking brakes, adjustable seats, and toe brakes with two exceptions, c/n 312 and 355. The exceptions were the last civilian STs built and were equipped as an ST-1.

Fillets, fairings and cowls were compound curved parts and those on the prototype were made with lead and plaster dies. The salt bath method was used to anneal the metal and then it was formed using individual sets of dies. In about 30 minutes it would harden itself to full strength. Some of the construction photographs show wooden patterns hanging on the wall; these were reproductions of various sections of wheel pants, bulkheads, etc., and were used to make the forming dies. The production dies were made of zinc and produced a very precise forming.

RYAN

The first ST, with a metal propeller and B4 engine, NC14223, c/n 101.

The first STA, NC14910, c/n 103, with Menasco C4 engine.

RYAN

Maintenance Notes for ST-1 and ST-2

Maintenance manuals for the early Ryans are incomplete and mostly cover only the obvious. The engine manuals are much better. Copies of these publications are readily available from a number of sources. The fact that there are no AD notes on any of the Menasco engines used or the two airframes does not mean that problems have not been found. The Ryan Company issued 32 Service Bulletins on Models 1 and 2 ST Ryans. To cover these adequately in this publication would be impossible.

An example of a Service Bulletin would be Number 12 issued April 23, 1940. It pertains to a retaining chain on the baggage compartment door, preventing it from opening more than five inches. If this chain breaks, the door will open to the point at which it interferes with the front control stick. The aircraft at this time will be completely out of control and in a dive. An STA, c/n 159, NC17354, came to an end because of this chain and crashed in April, 1940, at Minneapolis. The pilot parachuted to safety.

One of the most dangerous situations is that covered by Bulletin Number 31. During rolling maneuvers, the unsupported rudder and elevator cable turnbuckles because of centrifugal force, catching on the web of bulkhead #8, at the tail. Once caught, it becomes virtually impossible to correct the situation and the plane will most certainly crash. The safeguards against jamming are phenolic rub strips wired to the turnbuckles, presenting only a smooth surface to the offending web.

Many of these service bulletins cover items that are incorporated in the manufacture of later aircraft. Others are modifications of earlier service bulletins. A number of these are extremely important, particularly to the Ryan pilots who do acrobatics.

There are 43 engine bulletins issued by the Menasco Manufacturing Company. These, again, are an important aid in keeping the Menasco Ryans flying. Unfortunately, a large number call for parts and kits no longer available even though the Menasco Company is still very much a going concern.

One bulletin of particular interest is Number 1, Subject: Spark Plug Reach. The D4 and D4-87 engines need a long reach plug, and the one called for in the manual is no longer manufactured. In addition to this, most Ryans today have shielded ignition. The two types of plugs now needed, according to Champion, are, B-86N unshielded and REB 37 E shielded.

One change has proven to be a very bad conversion. It is Number 29 calling for two oil rings on each piston in place of one in the original equipment. This was found necessary because the engines were burning too much oil as a result of inefficient oil scraper rings. The rings manufactured today are much better than those of 30 years ago, and the result is that too much oil is removed from the cylinder walls. Compression rings then work on dry walls, and lose compression and then power. More wear and heat result, and the problem is hard to diagnose. The best repair is to replace all pistons, pins and rings, which are all currently available.

Many ST Ryans are exceptionally squirrelly and temperamental to land on hard surface runways. They are found to be rigged correctly according to the manual. But the book does not go far enough. Two other factors not covered cause much of this problem.

The first is the oil packing in the landing gear Cleveland Air Oil Strut. This cotton seal should be about three inches thick, holding each strut so they fall in flight to the same length, with no weight on them. If they differ in length or amount of oil, the wheel touching the pavement first will drag the aircraft in that direction, starting a potential ground loop. Also, if this packing is kept in good condition, it will prevent water from entering the strut and keep the oil in.

The second factor in taming the ST on landing is to equip it with bald tires. This was original equipment anyway. The bald tires will actually skid a little even on concrete making it much easier to handle.

The original 18" x 8" x 3" tires have not been manufactured since 1952. A number of years ago, an STC was issued for wheel adapters for this three inch hub so it will accept the standard Cub tire 800 x 4. These, with the new manufactured smooth tires, are excellent equipment.

One modification found on Menasco Ryans is an oil shut off valve. It is installed on the in line to the oil pump, and must be manually turned on before starting the engine. If the plane does not have a valve and sits a long time, the engine oil will seep from the tank through the pump, into the sump, down the cylinder walls and into the combustion chambers.

Hydraulic lock is one problem, but not the bad one. The uninformed pilot might fill his oil tank, relieve the hydraulic lock and start his engine and takeoff. He would be in trouble as the engine driven oil pump will then try to put five gallons of oil into a three gallon tank. It will not work, and the tank will split, spilling all the oil.

Irwin Hirsh was flying NC14986, c/n 118, over Lake Michigan in 1954 when his oil tank ruptured. His recollection of the incident is that he was nearly ten miles from Sky Harbor when the tank let go, dropping the Menasco's oil pressure slowly to zero. The engine continued to run but with increasing internal noise all the way to a safe landing. The engine was checked carefully after repairs to the tank and a refill of oil. The damage internally was so slight that the Menasco continued in service without a teardown.

In the last few years, a number of aircraft have been returned from Australia. These planes are equipped with Bendix magnetos SFR4-9. Although they have the same markings on the data plate, they internally fire in a different order from that shown in the owner's manual. They can be made to fire the same as other original equipment by replacement of the cylinder with a new one. This is not really necessary as long as the mechanic maintaining these planes knows of the situation.

The most common failures in recent years have been associated with magneto coils and condensers. Hard starting, particurly when hot, is frequently the first indication. I removed and had tested hot all my spare Bendix coils and condensers and found only two coils that performed well and none of the condensers of the nine pairs tested. In the particular case of my Ryan, c/n 177, it was found that both coils were satisfactory but the condensers were of the wrong micro farad value.

The Canadian propeller hubs are far superior to original equipment. These hubs are splined to their back plate, and are made for a propeller 3/32 of an inch thinner at the hub. To use these hubs, one must plane off the extra thickness of wood, or the splines will not close flush and proper clearance will not be maintained between the hub and engine. Also, because the hub is shorter, modification Service Bulletin Number 10 must be incorporated or you will bottom your crank shaft threads before you seat the centering cone on the hub.

Propellers are something that few people think much about. The difference in performance from one make or model to another can be significant. The propeller most commonly encountered on an STA is a 80R70 Sensenich. The STC for this prop is flexible and can be ordered as an 80 inch blade, 69-71° right hand rotation.

Early on I owned an STA, c/n 198, with a Menasco D4 of 125 hp with a 80R69 prop. It climbed very well, but cruised at only 95 mph. My current STA, c/n 177, with a D4-87 of 134 hp and a Sensenich 80R70 originally cruised at 110 mph and then was re-equipped with a Fahlin D-732. The cruise speed dramatically increased to 125 mph, with only a slight drop in vertical speed.

The Ryan aircraft in the ST-1 and ST-2 series are certified to fly with Sensenich, Fahlin and Flottorp propellers only. This is important because seven Australian ex-Dutch STM-2 Ryans have entered this country and some are equipped with Perfectus Air Screws and Fitzsimons props which are not legal.

Carburetor heat units were not standard equipment on any Sport Trainer aircraft, but were adaptable by an optional Service Bulletin number 32 dated September 7, 1940. These units are for C4, D4 and D4-87 engines only, as the C4-S has no provisions for a carburetor heater and does not need one. Air entering the carburetor intake travels around all four cylinder heads on the supercharged model and is "hot" enough to prevent any trouble.

Ryan STA NC9E was flying at 4,000 feet above the Illinois countryside one cold February day in 1965. The pilot was very cold and to get the blood flowing again he did numerous slow rolls. This helped, but was not good enough, and the STA was put into a shallow dive down to somewhat warmer air. As the ship's speed increased, so did the engine RPMs. To prevent exceeding the engine red line, the throttle was drawn slowly back.

After leveling out at 1,500 feet the throttle was advanced, but the Menasco had iced up to the point that it was only windmilling. It had only been a matter of a few minutes, but luck was with them and a good emergency landing was made with no damage. Half an hour later, with the ice melted, the Ryan was back in the air with a much wiser pilot at the controls. When you think about this happening to an engine that the manufacturer designed and advertised as not needing a carburetor heat unit, it makes you wonder.

There is one weak point in the carb heat box valve. The steel "flop valve" has been known to break and drop over the air intake. This has the same effect as a choke, but the engine will continue to run. The only indication the pilot has would be a sudden drop of approximately 100 rpm. The valve is visible through the front of the cowl on those engines not equipped with an air filter. Part of the preflight should be checking this valve by sight or sound. Before starting the engine, pull the carb heat control and if the valve is OK it will make a loud clank, easily heard in the cockpit.

Many STA Ryans are equipped with automatic carburetor heat units which work in conjunction with the throttle. These have the hot air entering the carburetor at all times except full throttle. The Canadian order for Menasco engines also had an automatic spark advance as well as the automatic carburetor heat. The spark unit is not used on the Ryan installation, the spark control being manual.

One of the most common questions asked concerns the interchangeability of Menasco engines on the Ryan ST aircraft. Basically, all five available models (C4, D4, D4-87, C4-S and C4S-3) are adaptable on all ST-1 and ST-2 airframes. The first three engines need no airframe modifications or cowl changes. This is not the case with the supercharged engines being replaced by one of the others or vice versa.

The cowl, engine mounts, throttle linkage and radiator mounts are quite different and require extensive surgery. My old STA, c/n 177, has a C4S engine mount carrying a D4-87 engine. Even after all obvious changes were made, one very serious problem came up concerning clearance of the carb heat filter housing and the left engine mount support.

Half an inch clearance seemed enough, but on the first flight, the engine vibrations were sufficent to crack the manifold as the housing repeatedly struck the mount support. The interchangeability of the B4 Menasco is of no consequence, as the only ST originally equipped with this engine (c/n 117, NC14985, and still flying) has already been converted to STA configuration.

The early export STM-1 aircraft were equipped with C4S engines of 150 hp. The STM-2 shipped to China and Java were supplied with C4S-2 engines of 155 hp. The only difference was in the ratio of the supercharger impeller. The first type impeller was geared 9.6 to 1 and the later model for the sea planes and light fighters were 9.8 to 1.

The Menascos are a very smooth running engine in spite of their four cylinder in line set up which is inherently rough. The one exception to this statement is the D4-87. They have much heavier steel rods as compared with the polished aluminum rods of the earlier models.

All parts of the D4 and D4-87 engines are interchangeable. The only points to bear in mind are that all four rods, pistons and pins must be changed as a full set. Also, because of the change in compression ratio, the top ring will stop on the cylinder wall in a different position, requiring careful removal of any vestige of a cylinder ridge.

Few parts are interchangeable from C4 to C4S engines. The major parts *not* useable from one to the other are: crankcase, pistons, rods, accessory case, and manifold system including carburetor and supercharger.

There is a mounting pad for a starter, but the usual drive for the generator is in this engine used to drive the supercharger. A special mount was available for a generator.

Two particularly weak parts are found on the C4S engines. The tappet guides work loose in the crankcase and then turn, which will either break the tappet roller or bend the cam shaft. The other part is the cylinder head "ears" that support the rockers; they have a tendency to crack, but can be welded.

Menasco powered Ryans could be equipped with a starter and generator as factory extras. No record of a factory installation of these parts is available. Three types of starters and one model of generator were STC'd for the Ryans: the Haywood air starter, Bendix Y150 electric and the Bendix direct drive (not inertia) hand crank starter, along with the Bendix 307 generator. The battery is located in the luggage compartment.

A number of problems come to light when these units are installed. They weigh approximately 50 pounds. Furthermore, it is impossible to remove or install a generator without removal of the engine from its mount, and it is impossible to install a starter without removal of one magneto.

One word of caution, the Y150 Bendix starter is available in both directions of rotation and the most common ones as used on Warner and Ranger engines turn the wrong way for a Menasco. The rotation can be reversed in the motor, but a new set of planetary gears, clutches and striker plate are needed for the gear box. These gears and clutches are the same for the electric starter as for the hand crank units. Also, some of the early Bendix E80 starters had the same gears, clutches and striker plate. The E80 starter will fit the Menasco, but is not STC'd and there is insufficient room between the engine and firewall.

As of 1976, only three Ryan STA aircraft are equipped with electric starters: NC17364, NC17351 and NC18922. A few, noteably ex-military Ryans, are using the hand crank starters.

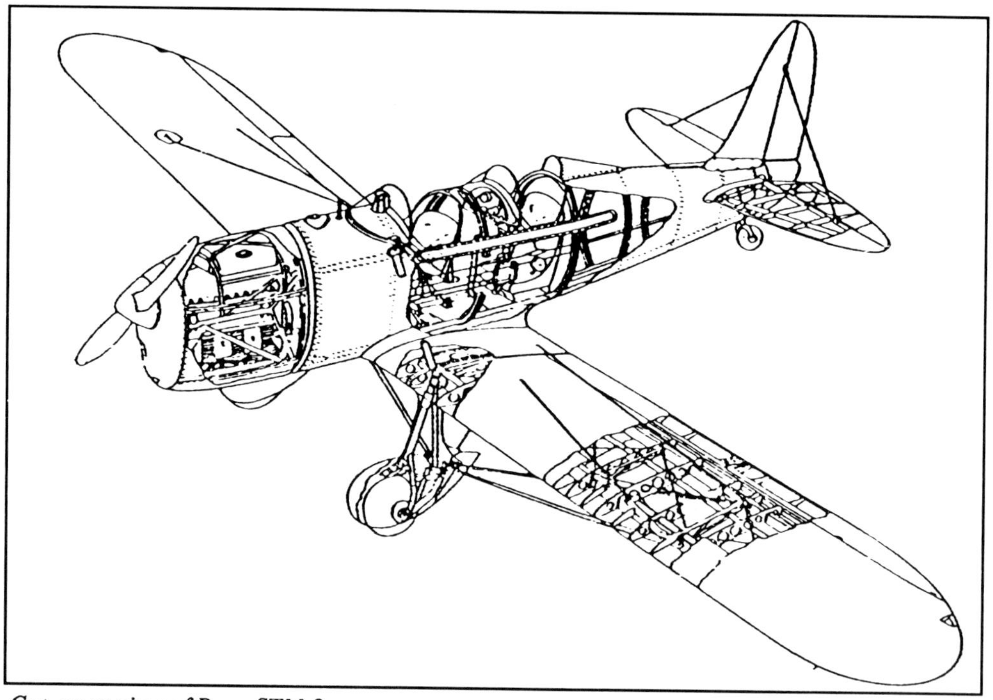

Cut-away view of Ryan STM-2.

Chapter Ten

Construction and Maintenance Details for ST-3

(PT-21, PT-22 and NR-1)

Construction Details for ST-3

The ST-3 series were a completely new aircraft in spite of similarities in looks with the early planes. They were strictly a military aircraft. If one phrase was to be used to describe these models, it would be "mass production military trainer".

Wings - Low-wing wire braced monoplane. Wing section NACA 2412, 4° 10' sweepback, 3° incidence and 4° 30' dihedral. Wing stubs are of riveted aluminum skin with a strut braced front spar, and cantilever rear aluminum spar. Outer wings had laminated spruce spars and stamped aluminum ribs of 24ST Alclad. The covering over the leading edge back to the front spar was aluminum with final fabric covering over all. Streamline tie-rods were used in the landing gear bracing. Ailerons and flaps were aluminum ribs and fabric covered.

Fuselage - Oval metal semi-monocoque, 3 inches wider than previous models. Structure consists of seven aluminum bulkheads, one steel and one that is half steel and half aluminum. The skin was made from six flat sheets of 24ST Alclad. The cockpit stringers were on the outside to make the openings as large as possible.

Tail Unit - Braced with streamlined wires. Aluminum alloy framework was covered with fabric. Rudder trim-tab adjustable on the ground. Elevator trim-tabs, operated from either cockpit with a crank; a position indicator was also provided. Elevators were counterbalanced. The rudder fairing was integral and fabric covered.

Landing Gear - There were fairings on PT-21 and NR-1 gearlegs, but not the wheels themselves. No fairings on other models. Cast aluminum treadle type gear with fixed position acting as anchorage for flying wires and widened 12 inches over previous models. Long stroke Cleveland Air Oil shock struts. Brakes were operated hydraulically, with toe type in both cockpits and the parking brake was mechanically operated from rear cockpit only. Steerable tail wheel with a locking unit. Navy variant was controlled from cockpit.

Power Plant - Kinner five cylinder radial engines on a steel tube mount. Three gallon oil tank in engine compartment.

Accommodations - Tandem open cockpits with complete dual controls and duplicate instrumentation. Adjustable seats adapted for the standard Army type parachute. Baggage compartment accessible from exterior only. Military three piece windshield.

Dimensions - Span: 30 ft. 1 in. Length: 22 ft. 5 in. Height: 6 ft. 10 in. Wing area: 134.25 sq. ft.

Maintenance Details for ST-3

A number of items have come to light as a result of experience that are not covered by the Maintenance Manual. The most obvious are the AD notes on the engine and airframe.

46-6-1 Front Fin Spar
46-6-2 Kinner Master Rod Repl.
46-6-3 Kinner Master Rod Knuckle Pin
51-28-3 Fuel Valve Placard

The ADs are self explanatory. The only comment about these which should be brought out is on the engine notes. A worn, but not broken master rod or knuckle pin leaves the unit in a condition that it can be repaired and modified so it will go on flying for years. But one which is broken cannot be repaired and the chances of getting another are becoming more difficult to find and expensive every year.

Propellers caused a lot of trouble because the CAA licensed some surplus 220 hp props, 90LA78. The result was that the little 160 hp Kinner had poor static rpm. This will sacrifice about 10% of the climb speed and almost all the acrobatic ability. There does not seem to be any loss of cruise speed with these surplus props. The propeller originally designed for the 160 Kinner is the Sensenich 90HA87.

PT-22, N46504, was a particularly good Ryan, with first class fabric, good paint, and a low time Kinner engine. It was my first experience with an ST. I held only a student license at the time and had heard all the stories about this "killer." An ex-military flight instructor, Jim Andrews, agreed to check me out if he were allowed first to "play" a little with the plane.

Have you ever flown cross country doing nothing but barrel rolls? Every approach for a landing was a falling leaf or an extreme slip. I had the hell scared out of me more than once, and in spite of the cold Illinois winter, there were many times when we returned to Waukegan with my flight suit wet with sweat.

One problem was that my Ryan would not loop, no matter what we did. With two pilots, two parachutes, and a half tank of gas, she would high speed stall or fall over on her back and spin inverted. Finally Jim went up alone and was able to do a poor egg shaped loop.

The propeller had to be the problem as everything else had been thoroughly checked. It was removed and gone over at the Whirlwind Prop Shop. We had two alternatives after identifying it as a 220 hp surplus blade. We could purchase a new one, or cut down the tips to give the Kinner more rpm and a "lower gear." The propeller was cut and balanced. This alteration made the difference, and my Ryan would now loop even with two aboard. We would lose altitude in a loop, but they were big and round and quite an improvement.

A bad accident occurred when the large aluminum casting forming the landing gear treadle broke. This casting is hollow and there is no good way of examining the inside without removal of the units from the plane. The problem is corrosion from the inside, weakening it to the point of breakage. Most of this can be eliminated by keeping the drain holes, located on the forward bottom side, free of dirt and open. At the same time the casting is examined, the hollow steel axle should be looked at since it also has the tendency to rust from the inside.

Back in the late 1940s through 1965, these planes were owned mostly by people who could not afford a modern plane. The situation is different now. A large proportion were painted to avoid the chore of polishing, and the paint jobs were copies of the then current Pipers and Cessnas. It was always an irritation at fly-ins to see judges awarding first prize to a well painted Ryan with a Cessna paint job and ignoring authentic restorations.

The flaps on a PT-22 are mostly for training; they give no lift and only a little drag. They can get you into trouble fast if the notches on the cockpit actuating pump handle slip when you are close to the ground. Rarely do they slip one notch, but rather suddenly go all the way. It is a simple job to make a new set of "teeth." Filing them will not work satisfactorily.

The Army did not like to "prop" its planes, and crank starters (not inertia) were incorporated. The Ryans are easy to start and the crank assembly is heavy (about 27 lbs.). It is best to remove both these parts. The crank is located in the luggage compartment on the ST-3. Four pounds of baggage were allowed and with the handle out, eight pounds were permitted.

Many Ryans have been converted to PT-22A configuration with the installation of a Kinner R-56 engine. These engines are heavier than the R-55 and lead weight must be added at bulkhead #8. A PT-22 equipped with an R-56, and with no weight bolted into the web of the bulkhead, it would be best to check out the weight and balance. The crank starter may have been removed, and this lightens the nose enough to eliminate the need for the tail weight. This computation must be made mathematically according to the aircraft manual.

The last item is the Holly 419 carburetor. It is not interchangeable from R-55 (R 540-1) to an R-56 (R 540-3). They can be set up for either engine by a qualified mechanic who has the carburetor specification and the test equipment needed.

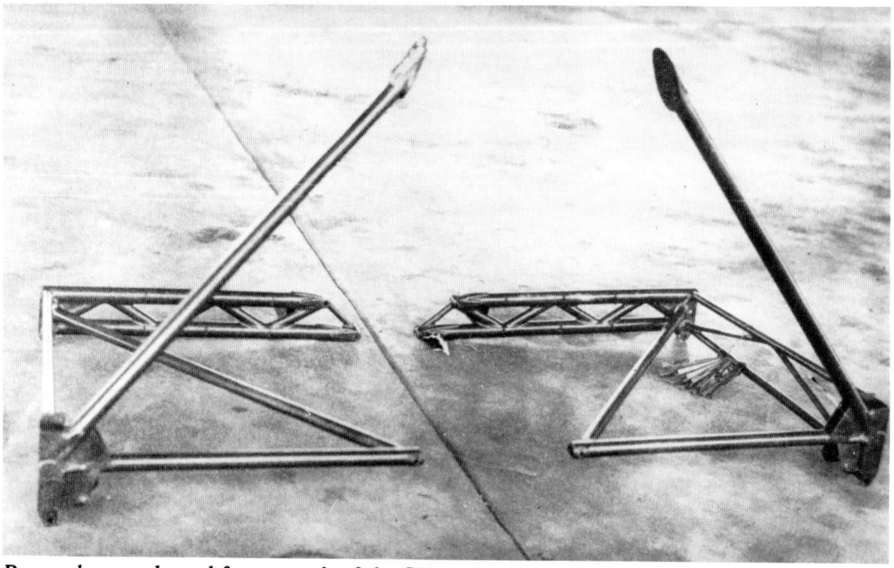

Rugged central steel framework of the STs.

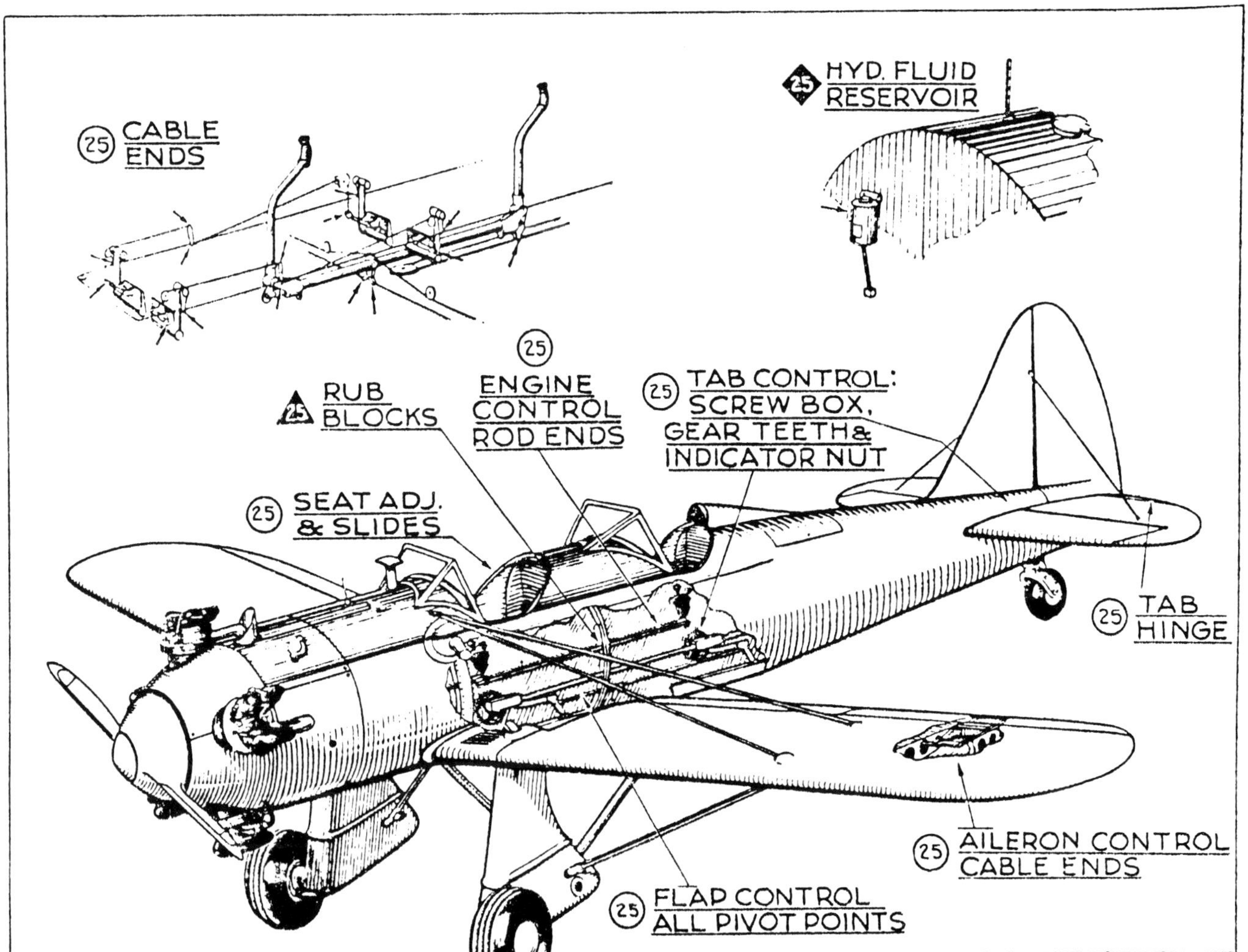

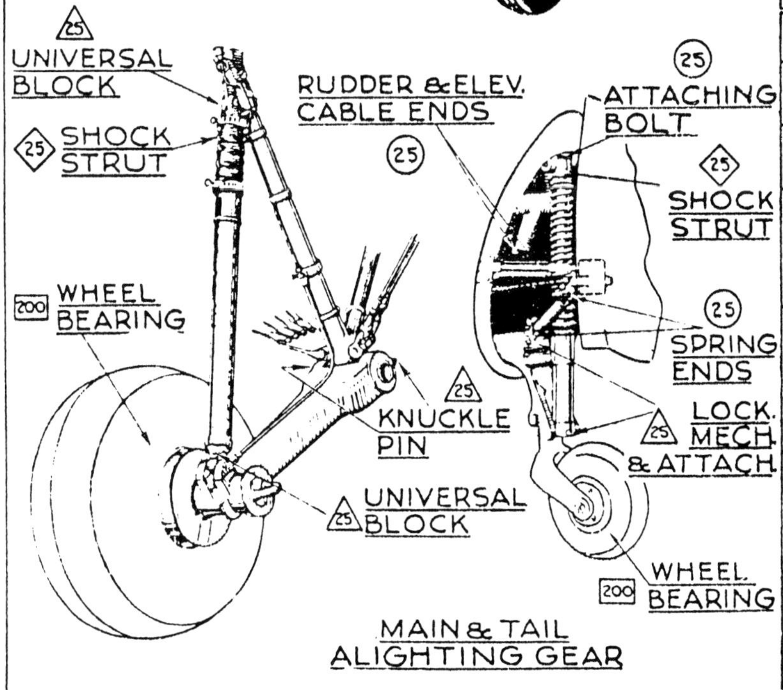

SYM.	APPLY	TYPE OF LUBRICANT
○	OILCAN	OIL 2-91 GRADE 98
▲	HAND APPLIED	GREASE VV-G-681 SOFT
△	PRESSURE FITTING	GREASE VV-G-681 SOFT
□	PACKING-SUMMER	GREASE, LUBRICATING, ALUMINUM SOAP, GRADE "B" MEDIUM. SPEC. AC 3581
□	PACKING-WINTER	GREASE, LUBRICATING. HIGH MELTING POINT GRADE 375 (SOFT) OR GRADE 275 (SOFT MED) SPEC. AC 3560
◇	OPEN HOLE	HYD. FLUID (MIN. BASE) STANAVO #9 OR EQUIVALENT TO SPEC. AC 3580
◆	OPEN HOLE	HYD. FLUID (CASTOR BASE) LOCKHEED #21 OR EQUIVALENT TO SPEC. AC 3586

NOTE:- NUMBERS IN SYMBOLS INDICATE PERIODS BETWEEN LUBRICATIONS - IN HOURS

FIG. - LUBRICATION CHART

PT-21 (ST-3)

Chapter Eleven

Construction Details for ST-4 (YPT-25)

Wings - Low wing cantilever monoplane. Two-to-one taper ratio. Wing incidence (root) 4°. Dihedral 5°. Sweepback (leading edge) 4° 03 mins. All-wood monospar wing structure in five sections comprising centre-section, two outer sections and two removable wing-tips. Structure consists of single wood spar, built-up wooden girder ribs, plywood-covered nose torque box extending from spar over leading-edge, and a final covering of lightweight fabric. Root ends of wing spar reinforced with hardwood blocks. Outer wing attached to centre-section at four points at spar root and one at leading-edge. All ribs, spar flanges and spar assemblies are brought to size from contour plates by routers and shapers to eliminate hand-finishing and to ensure accuracy with speed. Statically-balanced ailerons on outer section have wood spars and ribs and are fabric-covered. Starboard aileron has tab adjustable on ground. Electrically-operated perforated centre-section flap has wood spar and plywood skin.

Fuselage - Oval-section monocoque built up of ten laminated bulkheads and a stressed plywood skin. #1 bulkhead has black walnut plates at the four engine-mounting points. #2 bulkhead which carries torque tube joining leading-edges of outer wings has black walnut inserts at every other lamination. #3 bulkhead in three parts and is slotted to receive centre-section spar.

Tail Unit - Cantilever monoplane type. All-wood framework with plywood-covered fixed surfaces and fabric-covered horn-balanced elevators and rudder. Controllable tap operated from either cockpit in starboard elevator. Fixed trailing-edge tab in rudder for directional balance.

Landing Gear - Fixed cantilever type without fairings. Welded truss assembly bolted to centre-section spar. Long-travel oleo shock absorbers. Hayes wheels and hydraulic brakes. Oleo-sprung tail-wheel steerable from either cockpit, full swivelling beyond steering angles.

Power Plant - One 185 hp Lycoming 0-435-1 six-cylinder horizontally-opposed air-cooled engine on welded steel-tube mounting. Wickwire Spencer two-blade automatic variable-pitch airscrew. Two plastic fuel tanks in plywood cells in centre-section. Maximum fuel capacity 27 U.S. gallons. Oil carried in engine crankcase. "Eclipse" electric starter and generator.

Accommodation - Tandem open cockpits with complete dual controls and instruments. Streamline steel-tube turn-over post between cockpits bolted to centre-section spar. Safety seatbelts and shoulder harness. Blind-flying hood. Full night-flying equipment. Baggage compartment behind rear cockpit with access from within cockpit.

The above patch was worn on the back of the mechanic's overalls.

Specifications of the Ryan Sport Trainer

Model	Span	Length	Height	Wing Area	Power Loading	Empty Wt.	Gross Wt.	Useful Wt.	Fuel Gals.	Engine	Horsepower
ST	29' 11"	21' 5 3/8"	6' 11"	124'	16.6 lb/hp	1023	1575	552	24	Menasco B4	125 hp
STA	29' 11"	21' 5 3/8"	6' 11"	124'	12.6 lb/hp	1023	1575	552	24	Menasco C4	125 hp
STA-Spl	29' 11"	21' 5 3/8"	6' 11"	124'	10.5 lb/hp	1058	1575	517	24	Menasco C4S	150 hp
STB	29' 11"	21' 5 3/8"	6' 11"	124'	12.6 lb/hp	1023	1575	552	42	Menasco C4	125 hp
STW-125	30' 0"	21' 3 1/2"	7' 1"	124'	12.6 lb/hp	1042	1575	533	24	Warner SC	125 hp
XPT-16	30' 0"	21' 5 3/8"	6' 11"	124'	12.8 lb/hp	1023	1600	552	24	Menasco C4 L-365-1	125 hp
YPT-16	30' 0"	21' 5 3/8"	6' 11"	124'	12.8 lb/hp	1023	1600	552	24	Menasco C4 L-365-1	125 hp
PT-16A (STK)	30' 0"	20' 11 5/8"	7' 6"	124'	13.2 lb/hp	1060	1650	590	24	Kinner B5 R-440-1	125 hp
PT-20	30' 0"	21' 5 3/8"	6' 11"	124'	13.2 lb/hp	1050	1650	600	24	Menasco C4 L-365-1	125 hp
PT-20A	30' 0"	20' 11 5/8"	7' 6"	124'	13.2 lb/hp	1062	1650	588	24	Kinner B5 R-440-1	125 hp
PT-20B	30' 0"	21' 5 3/8"	6' 11"	124'	13.2 lb/hp	1050	1650	600	24	Menasco D4	125 hp
STM-1	29' 11"	21' 5 3/8"	6' 11"	124'	10.5 lb/hp	1058	1575	517	24	Menasco C4S	150 hp
STM-2	29' 11"	21' 5 3/8"	6' 11"	124'	10.2 lb/hp	1064	1575	511	24	Menasco C4S-2	155 hp
ST-3KB	30' 1"	22' 6"	6' 10"	134.25'	14.6 lb/hp	1255	1825	570	24	Kinner B54	125 hp
PT-21	30' 1"	22' 6"	6' 10"	134.25'	13.8 lb/hp	1278	1825	547	24	Kinner L-440-3	132 hp
NR-1	30' 1"	22' 6"	6' 10"	134.25'	14.09 lb/hp	1278	1860	582	24	Kinner L-440-3	132 hp
ST-3KR	30' 1"	22' 6"	6' 10"	134.25'	11.4 lb/hp	1272	1825	553	24	Kinner R-55 R-540-1	160 hp
PT-22	30' 1"	22' 6"	6' 10"	134.25'	11.6 lb/hp	1307.5	1860	552.5	24	Kinner R-55 R-540-1	160 hp
PT-22A	30' 1"	22' 6"	6' 10"	134.25'	11.6 lb/hp	1297	1850	553	24	Kinner R-55 R-540-1	160 hp
PT-22C	30' 1"	22' 6"	7' 2"	134.25'	11.6 lb/hp	1307	1860	553	24	Kinner R-56 R-540-3	160 hp
STM-S2	29' 11"	22' 8 1/2"	7' 4 1/2"	124'	11.8 lb/hp	1311	1828	517	24	Menasco C4S-2	155 hp
ST-3S	30' 11"	23' 7 5/8"	8' 5"	134.25'	12.6 lb/hp	1474	2021	546	24	Kinner R-55	160 hp
YPT-25 (ST-4)	32' 10 1/2"	24' 3 1/4"	6' 7 3/4"	161.2'	9.7 lb/hp	–	1800	–	27	Lycoming 0-435-1	185 hp

Performance of the Ryan Sport Trainer Data Table

Model	*Max. Speed*	*Cruise Speed*	*Stall-flaps No flap*	*Service Ceiling*	*Rate of Climb*	*Range Miles*	*Date First Mfg.*	*No. Built*	*Remarks*
ST	140	100	42/45	15,500	800 fpm	260	6-8-34	5	Under powered
STA	150	120	42/45	17,500	1,200 fpm	250	5-21-35	71	Small cockpits & heel brakes
STA-Spl	160	130	42/45	21,000	1,400 fpm	240	5-30-36	11	Small cockpits & heel brakes
STB	150	120	42/45	17,500	1,200 fpm	400	11-6-35	1	Aux. fuel tank in place of front seat
STW-125	150	120	42/45	16,500	1,100 fpm	240	3-12-40	(2)	Modified with Warner-engine tests
XPT-16	150	120	42/45	17,500	1,200 fpm	250	6-6-39	1	Originally civilian STA, NC18907
YPT-16	150	120	42/45	17,500	1,200 fpm	250	7-26-39	15	Service test aircraft
PT-16A (STK)	135	110	45/48	14,500	900 fpm	240	1-2-41	(14)	Converted to Kinner engine
PT-20	150	120	42/45	17,500	1,200 fpm	250	12-12-39	30	Model-2 airframe, large cockpit, toe brakes
PT-20A	135	110	45/48	14,500	900 fpm	240	10-7-40	(27)	Converted to Kinner engine
PT-20B	150	120	42/45	17,500	1,200 fpm	250	12-3-40	(2)	Converted to Menasco D4
STM-1	160	130	42/45	21,000	1,400 fpm	240	2-2-38	22	Military Model-1 airframe
STM-2	162	132	42/45	21,000	1,650 fpm	240	10-18-40	60	Model-2 airframe on wheels
ST-3KB	123	105	62/64	11,900	680 fpm	210	10-1940	1	Prototype
PT-21	123	105	62/64	11,900	680 fpm	210	1941	100	Landing gear fairings
NR-1	123	105	62/64	11,900	680 fpm	210	1941	100	Navy version landing gear fairings
ST-3KR	129	110	62/64	15,800	860 fpm	205	1940	1	Civilian ATC 749
PT-22	129	110	62/64	15,800	860 fpm	205	1941	1023	Originally built with Kinner R-55 engine
PT-22A	129	110	62/64	15,800	860 fpm	205	–	25	Originally ordered by the Dutch
PT-22C	129	110	62/64	15,800	860 fpm	205	1942	(250)	Field modified to R-56 engine
ST-3S	113	99	65/72	9,850	588 fpm	190	–	3	Prototype NX18924 not counted in no. built
STM-S2	122	108	55/59	12,250	700 fpm	220	12-7-40	48	Model-2 on Edo twin floats
YPT-25 (ST-4)	149	134	-/-	20,300	1,590 fpm	378	1942	5	Built for tests only. Never used in service

Ryan Sport Trainer
Manufacturer's List
Construction Number, Engine, Comments

C/N	Model	ID	Engine	Horsepower	Comments
101	ST	(NC14223)	B4	95 hp	
102	ST	(NC14909)	B4	95 hp	
103	STA	(NC14910)	C4	125 hp	
104	ST	(NC14911)	B4	95 hp	
105 to 179	STA		C4	125 hp	c/n 109 was STB, NC14953 c/n 117 was an ST with B4 c/n 173 and 174 were STA-Spls c/n 126 exported to Brazil
180 and 181	STA-Spl		C4S supercharged	150 hp	
182 to 187	STM-1	(Mexico)	C4S	150 hp	Invoiced December 9, 1937 First Military order MAF Field numbers 1-6
188	STA-Spl	(Civil)	C4S	150 hp	
189 to 191	STM-1	(Honduras)	C4S	150 hp	Invoiced May 31, 1938 Armed with single Machine gun *on* fuselage Field numbers 23, 24, 25
192 to 197	STM-1	(Guatemala)	C4S	150 hp	Fiedl numbers 23-26
198	STA	(NC18902)	C4	125 hp	
199	STA-Spl	(NC18905)	C4S	125 hp	
200	STM-1	(Ecuador)	C4S	150 hp	
201 to 214	Assigned to Ryan SC cabin planes				
300 to 305	STM-1	(Guatemala)	C4S	150 hp	Invoiced December 9, 1938 Machine gun mounts on wings, MC mounts for prior order 192-197 GAF field number 27-33
306	XPT-16	(U.S. Army)	C4	125 hp	Invoiced June 6, 1939, Originally civil aircraft NC18907
307 to 311	YPT-16	(U.S. Army)	C4	125 hp	Y designated service test Converted to PT-16A, January/April 1941
312	STA	(Civil-NC18922)	C4	125 hp	
313 to 321	PT-16	(U.S. Army)	C4	125 hp	Converted to PT-16A, January/April 1941
322	STA	(Civil-NC18923)	C4	125 hp	
323 to 328	PT-20	(U.S. Army)	C4	125 hp	Airframe is Model-2 Converted to PT-20A October/December 1940
329 to 338	PT-20	(U.S. Army)	C4	125 hp	Converted to PT-20A , October/December 1940 c/n 337 was a PT-20, used for Warner engine tests c/n 338 was a PT-16, used for Warner engine tests
339	STA-Spl	(Civil NC18921)	C4S	150 hp	
340 to 351	PT-20	(U.S. Army)	C4	125 hp	Converted to PT-20A , October/December 1940
352 to 354	PT-20	(U.S. Army)	C4	125 hp	Converted to PT-20A , October/December 1940
355	STA	(Civil-NC9)	C4	125 hp	
357 to 405	STM-2	(China order)	C4S-2	155 hp	Invoiced November15, 1939, 48 primary two-place trainers 2 single-place pursuit trainers (one MC *in* fuselage) Field number R1-R50
406	STK-1	(NX18924)	B5	125 hp	Factory test aircraft Disposition, included in China order (presumption)
407 to 514	STM-2	(Dutch order)	C4S-2	155 hp	Five contracts, June/Oct 1940 84 landplanes trainers (STM-2), 24 seaplane trainers (STM-S2) Dutch Army field numbers RO-10 to RO-69 Dutch Navy number S-11 to S-58 (land and sea)

Ryan NR-1 aircraft at the Jacksonville Naval Air Station 1942.

RYAN

Models ST-3KR/PT-22
Construction Number Detail

Construction Number	Model	Number mfg.
1000	ST-3	1
1001	ST-3KR	1
1002 - 1059	PT-21	58
1060	NR-1	1
1061 - 1076	PT-21	16
1077 - 1080	PT-22	4
1081 - 1154	NR-1	74
1155 - 1180	PT-21	25
1181 - 1205	NR-1	25
1206 - 1774	PT-22	569
1775 - 1799	PT-22A	25
1800 - 2248 *	PT-22	451
	Total	1,250

*Includes c/n 1979A

Navy Bureau of Aeronautics
Numbers of Model NR-1

Construction Number	BuAer No.
1060	4099
1081/1154	4100/4173
1181/1205	4174/4198

Army Air Corps
Serial Numbers

Model	Number mfg.	Serial number
XPT-16	1	39-717
YPT-16	15	40-40/54
PT-20	30	40-2386/2416
PT-21	100	41-1881/1980
PT-22	1,023	41-15173/15745
		41-20591/21040
PT-22A	25	42-57479/57503
YPT-25	5	42-8703/8707

Chapter Thirteen

About Al Menasco

RYAN AERONAUTICAL LIBRARY

Albert "Al" S. Menasco, founder of Menasco Motors and designer of the Menasco C-4 in-line engines which powered early models of the Ryan ST. Al Menasco, on the left, points out features of the Menasco C-4 engine. Claude Ryan is at the right.

Name — Albert Sidney Menasco
Place of Birth — Los Angeles, California
Date of Birth — March 17, 1897
Parents — James Buchanan and
Sophia (Waters) Menasco
Married — Gladys James of Los Angeles, 1920
Pilot Record — Learned to fly in Nigata, Japan, 1916
Military Record — 1917 Pilot, Canadian R.F.C.
1918 Aviation engineer, U.S. Army, Langley Field
Aviation Business Record — 1915-1917 Mechanical Engineer, exhibition flyer, aircraft construction.
1918-1919 — Service Rep, Wright-Martin Hispano-Suizo engines
1926-1932 — Founder, President, Menasco Motors
1932-1938 — President, Menasco Mfg. Co.

Information obtained from the 1942/43 edition of Who's Who in Aviation

Photo Album

Early Ryans

RYAN

Ryan "Standard"
The first ten airplanes operated by T. Claude Ryan included a mixed bag of surplus World War I airplanes. There were several JN4-D Jennys, a Thomas Morse Scout and six Curtiss J-1 Standards. These were Ryan's first attempts at improving existing aircraft and the modifications varied from minor to extensive with the Standards getting most of the attention. The fuselage gasoline tank was given an airfoil shape and moved to the top of the wing.

Ryan "Cloudster" Airliner
Ryan needed a larger airplane for the Los Angeles-San Diego Air Line and found an ideal aircraft for conversion in the huge Douglas Cloudster. Built in 1920 by Donald Douglas (c/n 1) for a non-stop flight across the U.S.A., the Cloudster sported a 56 ft wingspan, was 37 ft long and had a Liberty engine of 400 hp. After one attempt in 1921 and after the U.S. Army accomplished the trip in 1923, Douglas' partner lost interest and the Cloudster was sold. Ryan acquired the airplane third-hand, assigned it c/n 9 and converted it into the flagship of the airline with 10 plush seats, cabin lights, carpet and ashtrays for the passengers. In 1926 the Cloudster was pressed into service carrying beer in Mexico. During a night charter between Tijuana and Ensenada the airplane was landed in the water instead of the beach. It turned over, and waves totally demolished it during the night.

RYAN

Ryan M-1 *with a 150 hp water-cooled Hisso A engine. Claude Ryan flew this airplane for the first time Feb. 14, 1926.*

H. J. VAN DER LINDE

Test pilot John Fornasero and prototype Ryan ST.

ED MORRW

Peter Dana (rear seat) and a friend in Peter's black and silver ST-A in which he made a lightplane transcontinental record.

WALT HILL

Ryan ST, N17349.

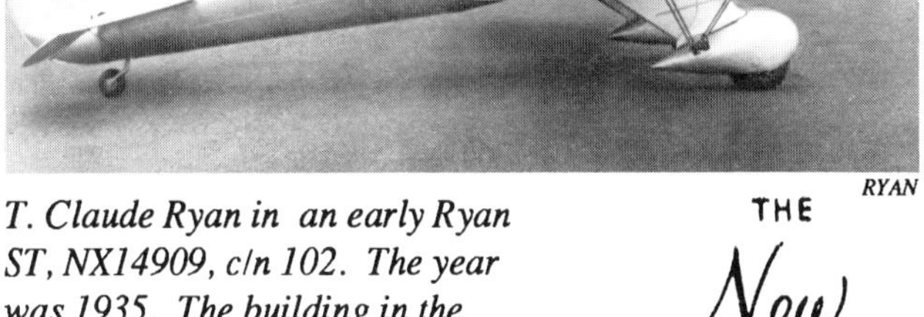

RYAN

T. Claude Ryan in an early Ryan ST, NX14909, c/n 102. The year was 1935. The building in the background was the school and terminal.

Ryan ST cockpits

THE New RYAN S·T

1941 Ryan STM-2 owned by Bill Rose, winner of EAA Trophey "Best Open Low Wing Monoplane" at Oshkosh 1983. TED KOSTON

Crack-ups

PT-21 (field number 80), "Crack up on field attempting to land" King City, 1942. BILL RICHARDS

Ryan PT-21 from King City, "Forced landing. broken crankshaft". BILL RICHARDS

Ryan PT-21s (field numbers 77 & 89), "Landing accident" at King City, 1942. BILL RICHARDS

A "Dodo," Navy student pilot, in a Ryan Trainer, "The Dodo," April 10, 1943. NAVY DEPARTMENT

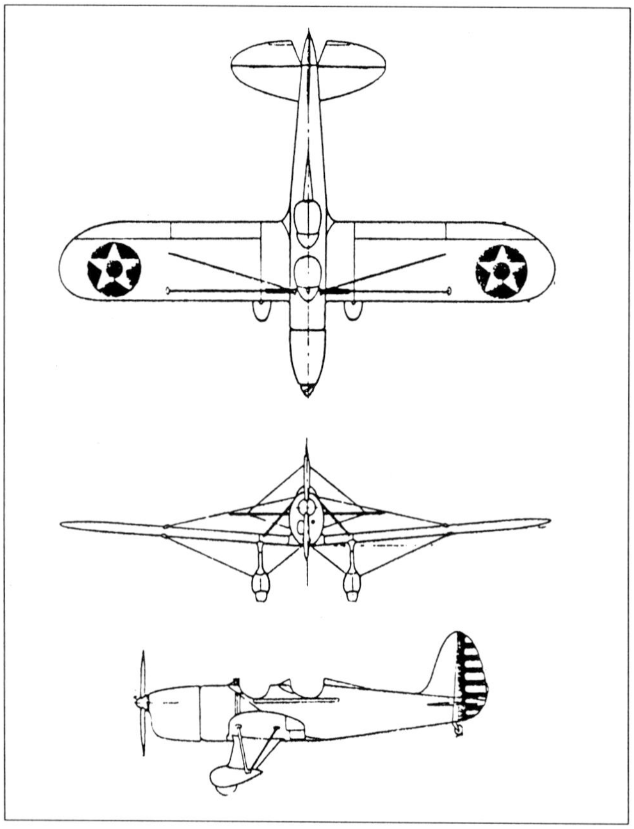

Ryan 3-Views

(Left) Ryan STM-2

(Bottom left) Ryan STM-S2

(Bottom right) Ryan ST-3

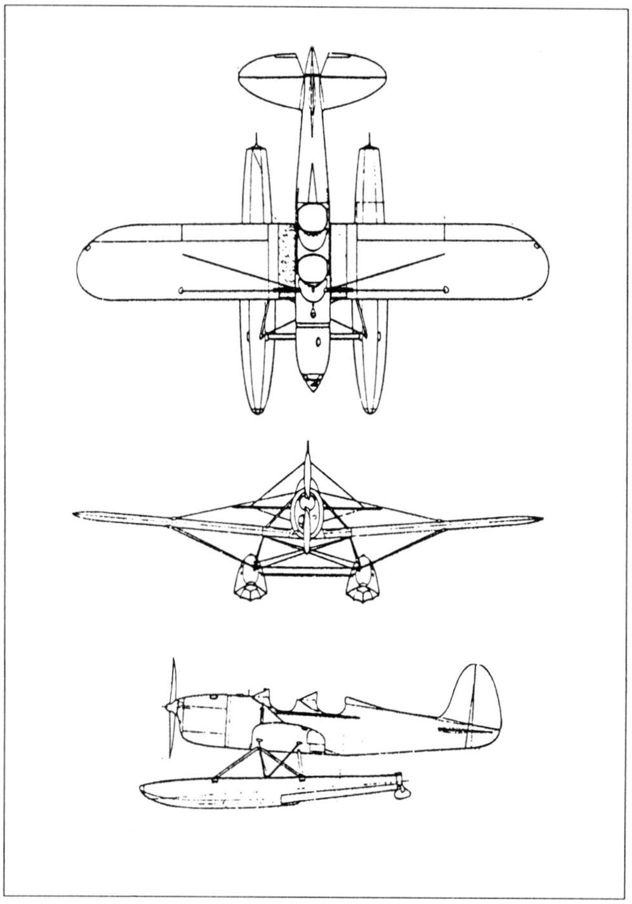

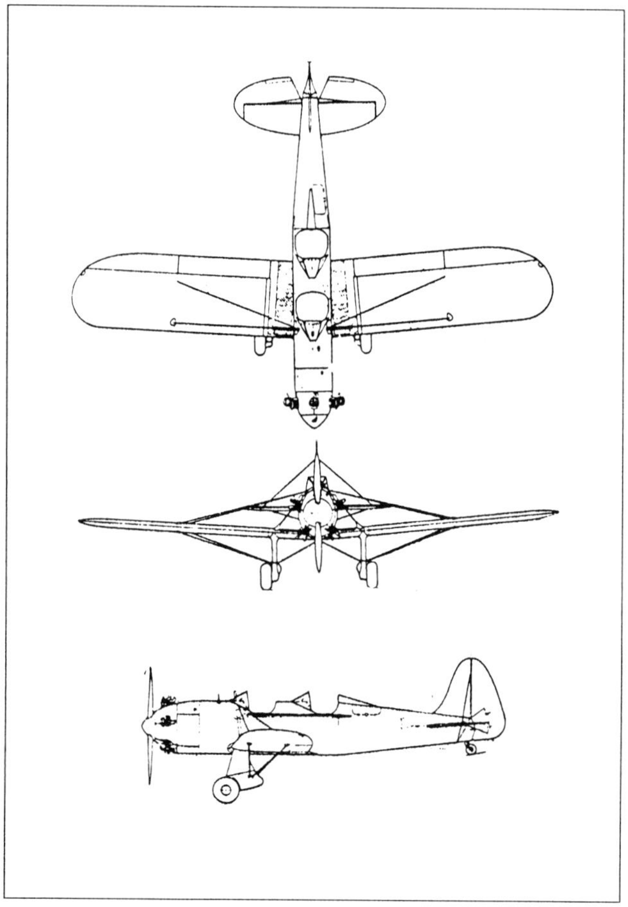